ADDICT AMERICA

The Lost Connection

DR. CAROL CLARK

ADDICT AMERICA
The Lost Connection

Copyright © 2011 by Dr. Carol Clark

Books may be ordered through booksellers Amazon.com
www.drcarolclark.com
www.createspace.com/3535496

Published by Dr. Carol L. Clark

ISBN-10: 1456505157
EAN-13: 9781456505158
Library of Congress Control Number: 2010919646

Printed in the United States of America

For
Don

CONTENTS

PART III:
RECOVERY AND CONNECTION

PART IV:
CONNECTION WORKBOOK

ACKNOWLEDGEMENTS

Thank you, Don, for your unfailing love and support,
for being my rock.
Thank you, Karen, my writing guru.
Thank you, Nicole, for all things technological.
Thanks to my family, who has been
the source of all my gifts.
Thanks to my friends and their unconditional love.

Thanks to the Universe, the Light, the Tree of Life—
all that we know as God—for always giving me
what I need when I need it.

This book was midwifed through the mentoring
process at hillhousewriters.com

PROLOGUE

MESSAGES

Shortly after my father died some years ago, I received from the Universe the first of several of what I have come to understand as messages about the meaning of life. For me, the Universe is what we think of as God. God is a word that holds many meanings for many people. It can be experienced as the Light, the Tree of Life, or any Higher Power. These messages began when I went to the town of Phoenicia in the Catskill Mountains to spread my father's ashes over the river where he had trout fished for all his life and probably had his own communications with his Higher Power.

Phoenicia is a significant place for me. I spent my closest moments with my father there and later fell in love with my husband amid its hills. The Catskills are also where Rip van Winkle fell asleep for twenty years. It's easy to believe that time can stand still among these weathered mountains that hold the wisdom of eons in their peaceful depths.

I chose to scatter my father's ashes from a forgotten metal bridge above the Esopus River. "His spirit has always resided here," I thought as I stood at the rail for what seemed like a very long time, just gazing at the water tumbling toward me from deep in the mountains.

I allowed myself to "just be" in this place that he and I had loved so much, and I began to open myself up to something larger than myself. Slowly I realized that I was asking a question about life and death. What was my life all about?

An answer surfaced as clear as a voice, but more as a visual thought. It told me to stop looking upstream and to turn around. I immediately understood that I had indeed been looking at my life from the perspective of where I had already been. But the past was something that could not be changed.

With this new insight in my heart, I turned around and crossed to the other side of the bridge. The water flowed away, out of sight, where it joined downstream with other bodies of water and eventually poured into the ocean. This represented my life. Like the water, I was moving forward toward an unknown future, joining with others eventually to be Connected in the sea of all life.

The next message that presented itself to me was "Do not fear." My questions about the meaning of my life had been related to my fear of the unknown! I had wanted concrete answers that would give me some sense of security, but instead I was told not to fear.

Standing at the railing, I noticed the beam of the bridge was a three-foot-wide arch, rising about fifteen or twenty feet above me. Normally I was afraid of walking out onto any midair suspension-type structure, but in keeping with the experiential nature of the message,

I decided to accept it as a challenge to face my fear and climb to the top.

But when I set foot on the metal incline and took a few steps, my fear overcame me. I froze. As I peered down at the rock-filled river thirty feet below and pondered what to do next, I realized that I didn't have to walk up the thing in order to get to the top. In facing our fears, we each need to do it in our own way, so I got down on hands and knees and crawled my way to the apex and sat down. Breathing in my accomplishment and feeling the exhilaration of overcoming my fear, I looked across the river and to the forest, letting the sacredness of the place absorb into my being. I sat for quite some time taking in the message I had just received and reflecting on the subtle simplicity of its meaning.

Ever since that day in the woods, this first message of "Do not fear" has been with me and has helped me through some of my darkest moments. Knowing that it came from something greater than myself gives me the faith to let my fears go—especially when they threaten to overwhelm me. When I need to, I visualize the river and crossing the bridge. In doing this I know that whatever comes, I will not be alone.

As time passed, I found more opportunities to open up to the Universe and receive messages. It became something that I could just do, but it always required me to find that part of myself that could "just be"—be at peace, without distractions and without specifically asking any particular question, but rather just being receptive, open. If I had questions, they were held gently in a pondering fashion. All I had to do was be aware of the message that was already part of me, since ultimately I am a part of all life.

My next message came when I was on the Key Biscayne Causeway with my dogs. This is a bridge of land connecting the mainland with the island near my home in South Florida. I had been living with a sense of expectancy and frustration, wondering yet again what my life was all about and worrying about what might be coming.

As I gazed at the Miami skyline just across the bay, I began thinking of Miami as being the place where I was going, my destination. I could swim across the bay to get there. It would be a short distance, but a difficult swim. The message now was that what was coming into my life was close, but I would have to put forth some effort to attain it. This gave me hope that something was coming soon, and since I've always worked hard, I felt it was something I could do. I was filled with hope and expectation! Something wonderful was coming my way.

Some months later, I travelled to New Mexico. The mountains there are newer than those in the Northeast, more rugged and sharp, rising high out of the dry desert. The air was clear as I sat on a rock in the sun, looking out across the valley to more mountains in the distance. I could feel my body connecting earth and sky as the energy of the Universe flowed through me. My mind once again opened up to receive a message.

When the message came, it was awesome in its simplicity. What came to me was: "This is it." Me, sitting alone on a rock, fully Connected to everything as every drop of water is part of the ocean, fully in the moment. I understood that this was, is, and always will be the meaning of life. Right here, right now, no hard tasks, no fear, no complex codes to decipher. This is it. It was the most peaceful feeling I had ever experienced.

As I write these words I realize how easy it is to forget the wisdom that has been given to me. How often do I take the time in my own life even now to "just be" and to allow my spirit to expand beyond my own consciousness? But when I remember to take the time to become Connected, my world falls into alignment like a camera lens bringing a picture into focus. We all get caught up in a past that can never be again and probably wasn't the way we remember it anyway. We worry about a future that may or may not come to pass and never will in quite the way we plan or anticipate. All we have is each moment of existence, and yet how easy it is to throw these precious moments all away thoughtlessly and recklessly, thinking that the next moment will be better.

I was content with this message of living in the present for quite some time as I practiced shifting my perspective from waiting for something wonderful to happen to appreciating what was happening in each moment. I read a passage in a Buddhist magazine that referred to the writer's observance of a monk as he crossed the village square. It was apparent to the observer that the monk was completely focused on each step, that his intention was to take the step and that was all that existed for him in that moment. Such attention and focus is almost incomprehensible to Americans. We seem to thrive on multi-tasking and take pride in our ability to focus on several things at the same time. A typical American crossing the square might be thinking about where he was going, whether there were any stones or cracks in his path, and maybe anticipating his dinner. He would be texting and e-mailing as he walked. This kind of all-encompassing stimulation is addictive, but more importantly, it keeps us *Disconnected* from the moment. Shifting attention to the moment is what shifts us into a place of Connection with the Universe—a place where all of our needs are met because all we really need is to not feel alone.

While working in my garden one day pondering the larger meaning of life, the meaning of human life, the insight came. Suddenly I saw all of us—all humans and animals, fish and flowers, all creatures great and small—as sparks of life, as individual lights. The lights were bouncing and twinkling, coming almost together then veering off, coming together in groups, then the groups bouncing about and finally coming together into larger groups. Each light was connected to the others as if by a thread of energy, the way the nerves in our bodies are connected. I saw the lights slowly coming together more closely, the vast cloud of them becoming more solid, more formed, more connected, until finally they were one light—one huge, glorious, blinding ball of clear white light! Every soul, every speck of life force, combined into a whole that was still only a part of the greater life force. This is my understanding of God.

This is the message that the great teachers throughout the centuries have been giving us—we are Connected, with a capital "C," and we cannot evolve spiritually on our own. Whether it is Jesus telling us to love and forgive everyone, Mohammed telling us to love one another, or the Dalai Lama rejecting nirvana to help others, the message is the same and the teachers are our models to show that only when all suffering is eased can we be without suffering ourselves.

When I received this new message and saw the lights come together, it was in answer to my question of "What is life all about?" I was content with that vision at the time, because I believed that my limited human mind could not take in anything more. Then, a year or so later, I began struggling with that concept again.

What about the ball of light? What would happen next? Was that it? Then I received the vision of the creation of the universe. As I considered the big bang theory, about which I had been reading in Bill Bryson's wonderful book *A Short History of Nearly Everything*, I saw the ball of light move beyond the universe to be the next atom that would explode into a new universe. It was so simple that I was amazed that I had thought it would be anything else or that it would be incomprehensible.

Raised in the Protestant faith (Presbyterian, to be exact) I had long rejected the Roman Catholic concepts of heaven, purgatory, and hell, but now I had a message that made these more clear to me in the context of Connection. With many religious constructs, there is a concreteness that is necessary to both make the construct easily understandable and to further the political ends of the religious institution. As any student of world history knows, the Roman Catholic Church is not only a religious institution but a political entity that, in the early days, wielded vast power and control over its members through such devices as keeping the Scriptures in Latin to prevent reading by lay persons, requiring that only priests could mediate between the laity and God, and by threatening excommunication (Disconnection) as the ultimate punishment. The receiver of such action was doomed to hell and a true believer of Catholicism would do anything to avoid such retribution.

The Catholic Church described heaven as being the place where those who professed repentance for their sins would go. Confessing one's sins to a priest who would then have the power to grant absolution facilitated this process. In addition, the idea of purgatory came into being. Purgatory is a sort of holding cell where a soul waits for entrance into heaven until enough people have prayed for the forgiveness of the person's sins. During the Catholic Church's first millennium and well into its second, it was a common practice for friends and relatives of the deceased to buy masses, or prayers, for the soul waiting in purgatory. Obviously the biblical saying "A camel can pass through the eye of a needle easier than a rich man can get into heaven" was overlooked here. A rich man could buy all the masses he would ever need no matter his sins on earth, and the church made a profit in the process.[1]

Even today, you will find candles in the church to be lighted with prayers for the departed and a donation box in the middle for that purpose.

For those who were beyond any absolution, either because they were unrepentant till the end or they had been excommunicated, hell was the place for them. The popular illustration of hell is a pit of fire, burning for eternity with Satan sticking his pitchfork into the tender portions of the anatomy of the sinners at regular intervals. (This may actually be more a fundamentalist Protestant depiction than Catholic.)

So today, as I was reading a book with some religious themes in the story line, I received another insight. The book contained a character who had sold his soul to the Devil. When he tired of his life on earth, however long he wanted it to be, he would move on to join his master. It came to me that if heaven, as I believe, is that place, that state of being, in which we are fully Connected and conscious of that Connection then hell is a state of Dis-Connect.

This led me to see purgatory and hell in a different light. Hell is not our time on earth when we are not acknowledging our Connection; it is that state when

---

1   In all fairness, the Catholic Church has often been, and still is, an agency that gives aid and charity to all. Their current difficulties have resulted in many cutbacks of desperately needed services to communities around the world.

we have put ourselves beyond any hope of Connection. While we walk the earth, there is always the possibility of redemption, of an awakening to our Connection and to the realization of the harm we have done others. That, I always thought, was hell. But now I believe that it is purgatory and that the Roman Catholic Church was onto this a long time ago. When we pray for someone, alive or dead, we are Connecting, we are putting our energy into them and feeling their pain. So purgatory truly is a place of waiting, since we are all in a sense waiting for the final coming together. When two lights come together, there is a sense of heaven, an experience, however fleeting, of that nirvana (the perfect peace of the state of mind that is free from craving, anger, and other afflicting states) for which we all long. Our glimpses of hell are those times when we are at odds with others, hurting them and denying our own hurt. It is through purgatory that we can Connect, forgive, and be forgiven and step into the light of heaven, for however brief a time.

When I have an inspiration, as I did today with the beliefs of the Catholic Church, I have the experience of having achieved a closer Connection to everyone who has ever held those beliefs. When any of us are cynical or dismissive of an idea, a belief, a group of people, a religion, or a culture, we can almost see the Devil gloating. Every superior remark or condescending put-down, every expression of hatred toward another person or group of people, makes it seem as though that final Connection is so far in the future we will be extinct before it can happen.

And yet we are living in such exhilarating times. A few years back, I was incredibly heartened by the phenomenal success of *The Celestine Prophecy*. It was not just about the message it conveyed, it was that it resonated with so many people around the world. I was uplifted in the Connection I felt with everyone else who had read this book. It was as if we were all being elevated to another plane, and it was the sheer number of people sharing that feeling that was so astounding. I felt hopeful for the human race in a way that I had not felt since the Age of Aquarius was sweeping our nation in the 1960s.

So what has this to do with addiction in America? Addiction is about filling that hole in our souls that is the emptiness caused by the loss of Connection. It is about running away from the pain of Dis-Connection. It is about distracting ourselves from the hopelessness we feel when we don't believe we will ever be Connected. It is about not being present, or not being in the moment, and it is about allowing fear to dominate us.

Paying attention to how we don't allow ourselves to "just be" and how we seem to deliberately find ways to separate ourselves from others can help us to make a choice to change. We can choose recovery, joy, and Light.

We can be Connected.

PART I:
ADDICTION 101:
THE BRAIN

WE'RE A NATION OF ADDICTS!

Obsessive, compulsive, out of control behavior done in spite of negative consequences to self or others—this is the definition of addiction.

This book is not about alcoholism or drug addiction. Plenty has been written about substance dependence. This book is about an addictive process that occurs in our brains as a result of the fast-paced, over-the-top, more-is-better culture in America—specifically the United States.[2] It is about how a myriad of other behaviors and activities have become addictive "substances" much the same way that drugs and alcohol are. Our brains respond to excessive stimulation, whether it comes from sex or cocaine, work or methamphetamine, food or heroin.

Americans have always prided themselves on being the biggest and the best, being fiercely independent go-getters. As a society we admire those who adhere to the "work hard, play hard" philosophy of life. This attitude has gotten us far and made us proud. Since the Revolutionary War for our independence, we have

---

2   The designation "American" has come to refer to people from the United States. Citizens of Canada and Mexico are more accurately "North Americans," just as there are Central and South Americans. The American culture of obsessive, compulsive behavior to which I refer in this book is something that is being exported around the world through media and technology. I will leave it to the citizens of the world to determine whether or not they want to identify themselves as part of "Addict America."

been pioneers, industrialists, inventors, and philanthropists. We live large and strive for the American Dream, whatever that means to us.

The down side of all this is that we are overworked, overstressed, overweight, and overindulgent. We spend so much time and energy trying to reach our goals of more—more money, more stuff, more power—we never stop and smell the roses. We never stop to "just be."

We are a nation of addicts, obsessed with wanting more, compulsively driven to get more, out of control with our behavior, until we destroy our relationships, our health, and our sanity. Above all, this drive to satisfy our more hedonistic selves has caused us to become Disconnected from our higher spiritual selves.

This book is about how we got here, what it means, and how we can learn to re-Connect with our inner spirit that knows how to "just be." Just be here, just be happy and content in this moment, just be with ourselves and with others, just be Connected to the Universe. Just be.

As you read this, do you feel anxious or relieved? Skeptical or hopeful? Disdainful or enthusiastic?

FROM SEEKING PLEASURE TO SEEKING RELIEF FROM PAIN AND DISCONTENT

Addiction begins with enjoyment and pleasure, so of course there may be a denial process about the negative consequences of addiction. Anxiety, skepticism, and disdain are feelings you might have if you do not believe you are an addict or if you do not believe that this view of the American way of life as addictive is accurate. "What's wrong with wanting more? Wanting a better life? Wanting to achieve?" you may ask.

While wanting more can be what motivates us to create a better life, this desire for more can keep us from enjoying the life we already have. When this happens, the discontent and emptiness we feel (negative consequences for ourselves and others) reside at the very heart of addiction. When you work twelve hours a day and then come home and spend more time working on the computer so you can earn more money for a bigger house and better car AND you are sacrificing time with your family and not slowing down long enough to "stop and smell the roses," that is obsessive, compulsive behavior. If even the *thought* of taking time to relax makes you feel anxious, your behavior is out of control!

The trick is in understanding the many aspects of negative consequences that are not always apparent. To be clear, a negative consequence is something that affects major life areas—health, relationships, finances, school, or work, and especially our sense of our spirituality.

How many times have you heard someone say to you (or someone you know), "You better slow down or you'll have a heart attack!" Stress is a negative consequence that causes any number of medical ailments, from ulcers to strokes to gastro-intestinal problems to heart attacks, and the list goes on. When stress becomes addictive, health problems multiply.

Negative consequences can also affect our relationships in broad-reaching ways. Harry Chapin, a popular singer/songwriter in the 1970s, did a song called "Cat's in the Cradle" about a father who never had time for his son's growing up because he was working too much. When the father finally retired and wanted to spend time with his son, the son was too busy with his new job and family to be with the father.

Partners who bring computers and cell phones into the bedroom because they cannot stop themselves from working are addicted. Their behavior (obsessive, compulsive) interferes with their ability to Connect with the person most important to them (negative consequences).

My own father was an alcoholic who, over the years, isolated himself from his family and friends before losing his health and his job. His life became centered on the bottle to the exclusion of all else. He was only interested in being with someone who would drink with him, and he did not want to do anything that prevented him from the act of drinking. I watched him go from being a talented artist and dedicated professional who enjoyed taking his kids fishing and camping to a man who sat in a recliner with a drink in his hand as he watched cooking shows—alone in his narrow world. He had lost all Connection with his wife, his children, and his friends. It was not until he was hospitalized with throat cancer and he went into recovery from alcoholism that he began to re-Connect with the long-buried warmth and love he had for his family and friends.

The negative consequences of addiction can also infiltrate our spiritual selves. It is incredibly easy for our lives to become so frenzied that we develop tunnel vision and make seemingly inconsequential compromises with our personal integrity. We all have that little voice inside us that tells us right from wrong. We call it a conscience, a superego, or a higher power depending on our particular perspectives. This voice truly reflects our awareness of right and wrong. When we explore this, we often find that at the base of our values lies that best of guides, the Golden Rule: "Do unto others as you would have them do unto you." This is at the heart of what this book is about, our Connection with others. Addiction cuts us off from Connection and lies at the root of our suffering. When we are Connected to others, we feel what they feel, so when someone is hurt, we feel their pain. When we love and forgive, we feel loved and at peace. Connection is the answer, but we can't get there without further exploration, so let's get back to our negative consequences for a moment.

Losing Connections

Think about wanting something to the exclusion of all else—money, power, pleasure (which are all interrelated). Let's say you're a work addict, or workaholic. Your life is about the big deal, about winning a contract, getting a promotion, making more money. You are obsessive and compulsive about this, thinking and breathing work 24/7. Your relationships suffer because you are never home, and when you are, you are working. Ethically you make compromises. A friend at your company has a great idea but you may present it as your own (Lost Connection). You make promises to clients that you know can't be kept (Lost Connection). You cheat on your expense account (Lost Connection). You pretend you like your boss when you really think he's a stupid ass (Lost Connection).

When you lose Connection you compromise your deepest held values. You don't spend time with your family and even blame them when they want attention, rationalizing that you are working hard for their sakes. You pull away from friendships and disengage from your chosen spiritual activities. You may even use drugs or sex as a way to relax, justifying yourself with the excuse that you work so hard you deserve a break. Every one of these examples is a compromise of ethics, which is a violation of spirituality and loss of Connection. Multiply each example over and over, add more of your own, and eventually you are in a quagmire of self-loathing from which you think you can escape only by compulsively doing more of the same thing and by more rationalization and justification. This is the cycle of addiction.

Addicts are not "bad" people. They are not inherently immoral, uncaring, or unethical. Quite the opposite, in fact, since one of the hallmarks of addiction is the shame and despair that is felt when they realize even a hint of the harm that results to themselves and others. But when addicts wake up to the negative consequences of their actions, they become willing to break through the Disconnection of denial and become Connected.

There have been several animal research studies that demonstrate the power of addiction and help us to understand how it is only through our human ability to reason and be Connected to our spiritual selves that we are able to overcome the chemical changes that occur in our brains. In these studies, animals are taught to press levers to be given food or water. Then they are given cocaine until they are addicted and then offered a lever to push to obtain cocaine. The animals will press the cocaine lever until they die of thirst and exhaustion. We're talking here about animals that will chew off their own legs to survive, but once they become addicted to cocaine, they lose their survival instincts and only crave the drug. It is only through our human ability to reason and our yearning for a higher purpose in life that we are able to say "Hey, wait a minute, this isn't working for me, this is not how I want to live, I want a different life!"

While on the one hand addiction is a barrier to intimacy and Connection (which is at the heart of the emptiness that leads to addiction), on the other hand, it can be the greatest gift of our lives!

Once we realize how addiction has controlled our lives and Disconnected us from love and intimacy and our higher power, we can then employ that part of our brain that can make a decision to move into recovery. Humans can make conscious decisions about what is really important in life. We can be more spiritual, more loving, more Connected, and experience joy every day. The energy we create brings more love and intimacy and Connection to us. This in turn spreads throughout the world with the very air we breathe, and the world literally becomes a better place.

Would you like to know more about how we can do this?

THIS IS YOUR BRAIN ON DRUGS

We have two areas of our brains—the limbic system (think "Caveman Brain"*[3]) and the prefrontal cortex (think "Enlightened Brain")—that optimally work in harmony, yet in addiction, their partnership becomes codependent and enabling (codependent meaning they are both engaged in perpetuating the addictive behavior and enabling in that the Enlightened Brain makes the excuses for the Caveman Brain to get high). The Caveman Brain contains those parts of the brain that have to do with survival, pleasure, and basic emotions. Those things that give us pleasure also allow us to survive—both individually and as a species. For instance, food tastes good so we eat and live. (Think about a time when you were sick and lost your appetite. You stopped eating.) Sex gives us pleasure and so keeps us alive as a species. If we don't enjoy it, we don't do it.

The exceptions to this occur when the Enlightened Brain intervenes. That part of our brain is where our ability to reason and use logic is housed. Our Enlightened Brain is what tells us to eat food to live even when it doesn't taste good or to have sex if we want to start a family even when we're not in the mood. It is what tells us to get out of bed in the morning and go

---

3 I use the word "Caveman" rather than "Caveperson" for conceptual simplicity, not out of sexism.

to work when we would rather sleep late and tells us to exercise when we would rather veg out on the couch. In other words, it intervenes to not just keep us alive but to have a better quality of life.

It is because of the Enlightened Brain that we are able to create long-term goals, maintain the needed attention to pursue those goals, and delay gratification in order to accomplish them. We can evaluate choices and plan the best course of action while learning from our mistakes. The Enlightened Brain translates the feelings from the Caveman Brain into recognizable words and emotions. For example, it is in the Caveman Brain where I experience the pleasure of eating chocolate and it is the Enlightened Brain that says "I really like chocolate!"

The Enlightened Brain is also where the awareness of our spiritual Connection to a higher power exists. This area of the brain houses our conscience and sense of empathy, our ability to interact positively with others and feel compassion. This relatively new (evolutionary-wise) part of our brain, which separates us from all other animals, is what makes us search for the meaning of life. It allows us an awareness of our own existence, which then leads us to be aware of others' existences and ultimately to feel the Connection—first to our caregivers, then to our families, then to our community, and on outward until we are aware of being Connected to all life.

While our awareness of and need for Connection to others and to all life is known to us through this part of our brain, the Enlightened Brain is also keyed into our survival through the Caveman Brain. From our time in the womb, we are Connected to our mothers and need that Connection for survival. When we are born, we develop a need to build more Connections, not only for our physical survival, but for our emotional health. Research has shown that babies who are not held or nurtured can grow up with difficulties in forming attachments to others that manifest anywhere from an inability to make friends to an inability to develop and maintain an intimate relationship all the way to criminal behavior. This fear of intimacy, or Connection, is a conditioned response to life circumstances.

There is also some interesting research that demonstrates the "shut down" of emotion and attachment when a caregiver disengages for even a few minutes. The study (using the Still-Face Paradigm, Ed Tronick) had a mother facing her baby and interacting with smiles and cooing and the baby responding in kind. Then the mother turned her face away and did not respond to the baby whether it smiled or made sounds of distress. Within two minutes, the baby lost all affect (the outward manifestation of mood) and appeared apathetic. In this study, the mother quickly re-engaged with the baby and the baby recovered energy and excitement. Imagine the consequences to the child if the mother did not re-engage!

Another series of experiments were made by Harry Harlow between 1957 and 1963 using rhesus monkeys. He took the baby monkeys from their mothers and put them each in a room with either a wire monkey form that had a milk bottle attached to it or a soft, terrycloth form that was huggable but had no milk. He also performed the experiments with terrycloth monkeys that provided milk. The monkeys were thus isolated with either a food source or a comfort source. In both cases involving the terrycloth surrogate, the baby monkeys clung to the surrogate whether or not it provided milk and even ran to it when a frightening stimulus was introduced. These monkeys were able to socialize and bond with other monkeys when they matured. The monkeys with food but no comfort surrogate grew up to be antisocial and incapable of forming attachments.

This is also what happens to us throughout our lives. We are conditioned to respond to stimuli, and this learning takes place in the Caveman Brain. For example, if a child is crying because he's hungry or wet and a parent immediately picks him up and holds him, feeds him, and changes him, the child will feel safe and comforted. If the child is left alone to cry, he will associate feelings of discomfort and distress with being alone and Disconnected. The child's Enlightened Brain will take that conditioning and try to make sense of it, try to find reason and logic in it, but as he does not have the context in which to do this (because the child has no life experience), he will come up with the idea that the world is not safe, that he is unloved and unwanted, and that his needs will not be met. The child learns that intimacy is to be feared because he is not loveable and the people he cares for will let him down.

Addiction can develop when a person realizes that he or she can escape the pain (often experienced unconsciously) of not feeling Connected, of not having intimate attachments. Some behavior—be it drugs, gambling, shopping, eating, sex, work, or video games—provides the pleasure that soothes and comforts and may even give a sense of power or competence to that inner child who was left alone. Over time, however, those behaviors are never enough, because they do not really address the underlying cause of the pain, and so more of the "drug" is sought in a recurring effort to self-medicate.

Connection is an innate ability! To be Dis-Connected is a dysfunction of our true potential. To lose Connection means our natural abilities have been disrupted!

What actually happens to our brains when we become addicted?

In the 1980s, when cocaine was rampant in the clubs and the social scene, people would say that it was not addictive because there was no physical phenomenon accompanying withdrawal as there was with alcohol or heroin. Then we discovered through brain imaging technology that cocaine addiction is very real indeed, and through better understanding of how the brain works, we have broadened our definition of addiction and better comprehend how we can become addicted to almost anything.

We can readily see tolerance—ability and need to ingest more of the substance to get the same effect— in the behavior of people around us or in ourselves, as in tolerance to tobacco or alcohol. Many of us can remember taking that first drink or puff on a cigarette and feeling the effects, but then quite quickly we found that we needed a whole cigarette or a couple of beers to feel good, then a pack of cigarettes or a six-pack. Our bodies and brains adjusted to the substance and so we needed more to feel the effects.

Through media depictions of addiction, such as the movie *28 Days* or the reality shows following people in rehabilitation programs, we can see the physical withdrawal from a substance, as when a heroin addict experiences nausea, sweating, diarrhea, and other flu-like symptoms when they try to quit "cold turkey," as it is called. Alcoholics experience the DTs, or delirium tremens, which are hallucinations and shaking, when they stop drinking after years of dependence. In advanced stages, the alcoholic actually begins withdrawal while sleeping and so wakes up in the morning with hand tremors. Or we can simply see the tension and agitation that builds when we or someone we know wants a cigarette. These are physiological symptoms of tolerance and withdrawal, which make up the basis of dependence.

But now researchers are learning about the chemical processes that occur in the brain when someone becomes addicted to other substances or even behaviors.

Addiction is about stimulation, and stimulation can come not only from drugs such as cocaine, but also from sex, gambling, computer games, texting, stress, anger, and work. We are exposed to stimulation all day, from every conceivable direction. Just as a caveman became highly stimulated when confronted with danger from which he had to fight or flee, modern man (and woman) is under stress throughout the day from the stimuli of their highly charged lives. Our brains receive signals from external stimuli and then release a variety of chemicals (such as dopamine, norepinephrine, enkephalins, and adrenalin) that cause the physiological effects of excitement and pleasure.

How do these chemicals really affect the brain?

The one we are most concerned with in addiction is dopamine, and the way it works is this: The brain is made up of neurotransmitters (senders) and neuroreceptors (receivers). Quite simply, the neurotransmitters acquire a signal, either from one of our five senses or from an internal thought (going on vacation or taking an exam), and send it to a neuroreceptor, which activates a response based on what kind of signal it receives. For example, when our nerves are stimulated pleasurably, as in sexual activity, the neurotransmitters release dopamine to the neuroreceptors and a feeling of pleasure is experienced. This response is programmed into the limbic system as it makes the association between the sexual activity and the feeling of pleasure.

When it is repeated a number of times, then just thinking about the activity can cause a feeling of pleasure. This is called "conditioning." The Enlightened Brain then uses logic and reason to make sense of the experience and give it a cognitive interpretation, as in "I am loved because my partner made me feel so good" or "I'm a stud" or even "I feel good masturbating on my own and don't need anyone." Not very enlightened, but it doesn't know about addiction yet. But back to the limbic system/Caveman Brain.

The limbic system is millions of years old and does not take easily to change. It strives to maintain the status quo and will take measures to do so. Therefore, when a person is stimulated to a greater degree than what the brain considers normal, which is evidenced by a greater transmission of dopamine than normal, the brain will shut down neuroreceptors so the amount of pleasure will remain stable. Furthermore, dopamine is normally recycled in the brain, but once the brain begins to adapt to the new levels of stimulation, it does not recycle the dopamine, so there is less available for transmission.

If a person is playing a computer game once a day, for example, then increases playing to several times a day in order to feel that same degree of pleasure with more frequency, the receptors will begin to shut down, leading to reduced pleasure as time goes by. Since the person expects to experience the same level of plea-sure, he or she will keep trying to attain that by playing more and more often or playing more sophisticated or different games to try to enhance the experience. For many people, playing the game is not only for pleasure, but for escape, and that is when the addictive pattern is firmly established. We all have something from which we want to escape—boredom, frustration, bad relationships, or painful memories. You can add your own to the list.

Addiction can occur when we either take an addic-tive substance in great quantities over a long period of time or when a substance is enhanced to provide greater stimulation in a shorter time span. The for-mer is a difficult way to become addicted; the latter is quite easy and is how most people today become ad-dicts. Think about it: when peasants in England were drinking cheap ale, yes, they could become alcoholics, but only after years of drinking *a lot* of cheap ale. The poorer urban folks in London had access to gin, a far more potent drink, and they became alcoholics with greater facility and more dire consequences. The ru-ral peasant might regularly get drunk on a Saturday night, but he had to go work the fields six days a week and therefore did not have the leisure to indulge in his addiction. The poor in the cities had more leisure time to indulge in their habits and were more likely to be engaging in criminal activities that gave them job flexibility, as well as the approval of their peers. The rich, of course, had access to the best liquor and plenty of time in which to indulge and so were highly likely to be alcoholics once they started on that path.

The addiction we see today is primarily the result of a substance being enhanced for the purpose of intensifying the stimulation. Tobacco was used by Native Americans for centuries without apparent ill effects. Along come the Europeans and the next thing we know, we're all puffing on Marlboros behind the garage and becoming cigarette addicts before we're out of high school. As we know from the plethora of lawsuits being won against tobacco companies, those companies enhanced the addictive effects of tobacco to enlarge their market. (One of the ironies of this is that many tobacco company executives, in their zeal to prove the safety of their product, became addicted themselves and fell prey to lung cancer and emphysema.)

Another drug that has been significantly enhanced is cocaine. Coca leaves have long been chewed or drunk as tea by the Andeans to help with the stress of high altitudes and often impoverished conditions. By changing coca leaves into the white powder we know as cocaine, the stimulative properties are enormously enhanced. Furthermore, the powder form allows the drug to be ingested either nasally or intravenously, which means that it will reach the brain far more quickly than by eating or drinking it. The effects also last less time, as the drug is able to enter the bloodstream in its entirety rather than through the slower process of being absorbed through the stomach.

What all of this means is that the person snorting cocaine will feel a tremendous rush of stimulation and euphoria within a few minutes of inhaling it and will get the full intensity of the drug all at once, but the effects will wear off in about twenty minutes, leaving the user craving more right away. This is why cocaine users will go through large quantities of drugs and money in a short period of time and why they also become addicted in a short period of time.

Compare this to alcohol. When a person drinks a beer or a mixed drink, the alcohol is absorbed through the stomach lining along with whatever else is in the stomach, so speed of absorption varies, but it will take many minutes for the first effects to be felt. Furthermore, only the liver can cleanse the alcohol from the bloodstream, and it does this at a rate of roughly one ounce per hour. As the alcohol continues to be absorbed over a period of time, the high will be prolonged. A person consuming several drinks can expect to feel the effects for several hours. Someone must put a lot of time into their drinking to become an alcoholic. As we know, many people do dedicate themselves to this, but it takes work.

In brief, then, how quickly one becomes an addict depends on the concentration of the addictive substance, how quickly it reaches the brain, and how quickly it wears off.

So how does someone become an addict when there is no substance causing the stimulation? Well you might ask.

Let's look at our caveman. He didn't eat, drink, inhale, or inject any substance. An external event triggered the brain chemicals to be released that caused him to become "high." He experienced a "natural high," which is what we call it when we feel a euphoric stimulation from exercise, love, or the presence of a saber tooth tiger. We seek out stimulation even from what we might label as a negative event. How many times have you heard someone say that they work best under pressure? Look at the numbers of people who flock to see scary movies. What about the friends who are always complaining that they can't find a nice partner but are going from one dramatic relationship to another?

We all have a mood baseline—the place where we feel neither good nor bad, happy nor sad, aroused nor depressed. This is the neutral place from where our limbic system measures our level of pleasure or depression.

When there is external stimulation, our mood changes. Stimulation is simply something that happens that triggers a response. It has no negative or positive qualities in and of itself, it only triggers a chemical response in our brains that may be modified by the thoughts or beliefs we associate with it. For example, I may be walking down the street and see a person walking toward me. This is the stimulating, or activating, event. My response is based on several factors—do I know this person? Do I like or dislike this person? Do I not know this person and feel afraid? Feel friendly?

Don't care? The belief or thought about this event then dictates the mood response. I may feel pleased, happy, or afraid or any number of other feelings. This stimulation will cause an upward departure from my baseline. As the stimulator recedes, my mood will return to the original baseline. The Caveman brain recognizes stimulation from whatever chemicals are released—dopamine, adrenaline, etc. The Enlightened Brain will interpret the stimulation as pleasurable or otherwise.

Imagine having sex and experiencing an orgasm (go ahead, take your time). The level of pleasure and excitement will rise sharply and then return to normal, or baseline. You go back to ordinary activities and then think with pleasure of the memory. Any stimulating event, memory of an event, or anticipation of an event will cause that mood elevation from the baseline.

Conversely, the absence of stimulation will cause depression. A downward departure from the baseline results in feelings of apathy, boredom, and sadness.

Drug use causes extreme fluctuations from the baseline. Snorting cocaine will cause a very high, sharp spike with a resulting crash that will cause a dip before returning to normal. As an example of how drugs affect the mood baseline, let's make a graph giving a numerical assignment to the stimulators. Note the contrast between a natural stimulant (such as an orgasm with an intimate partner) and an artificially enhanced one (such as methamphetamine). It is the craving for the enhanced stimulation that causes addiction.

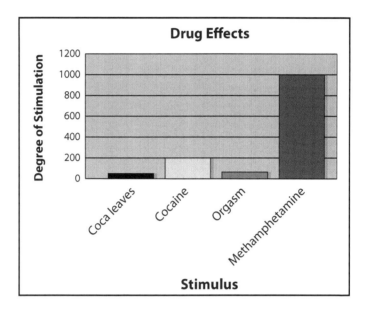

As the limbic system strives to maintain equilibrium and cope with the extreme stimulation, or arousal, caused by cocaine or methamphetamine, the brain will shut down the neuroreceptors that receive the stimulation in an effort to dull the effects. Therefore, it will take more of the drug, or more stimulation, to achieve the same effect. As the brain attempts to adapt, the baseline rises, resulting in the crashing going deeper and depressing the mood accordingly. Eventually the baseline is so high that the addict requires the drug just to feel normal and experiences severe depression without it.

Process addiction is what we call an addiction to a behavior, such as sex, gambling, or shopping. A person begins to elevate the level of stimulation, causing the baseline to rise and tolerance to develop. Any stimulation that is less than that required to register above the baseline is interpreted as depression, and the person becomes anxious and irritable and craves the stimulation that will allow him or her to just feel normal, as well as to reach a level of pleasure that will dull the pain. Some people, including therapists and psychologists, will say that process addictions are a myth, that sex, for instance, is a natural behavior that may be compulsive but that any attempt to call it an addiction is just a way to excuse a person's behavior or to be judgmental about that behavior. From what we know about dopamine neurotransmission and reception, however, this simply is not true. Specific sexual behaviors, as well as other behaviors that are obsessive, compulsive and out of control, are as much addiction as cocaine and alcohol dependence.

Furthermore, with brain imaging technology such as positron emissions tomography (PET) scans and single-photon emission computerized tomography (SPECT) scans, it can be seen how the use of drugs stimulate the reward pathways of the brain and how, when the drug is withdrawn, the activity is diminished to a level below that of nonuser, resulting in depression, irritability, and craving.

These scans can also show how, over time, brain metabolism is decreased. Newer brain imaging technologies can accurately identify those specific sections of the brain not functioning optimally and from that we know what functions are affected—memory, judgment, etc.

Thanks to recent research, we can now see this with process addictions as well. A PET or SPECT scan of the brain of a sex addict, food addict, or gambler will show the same lack of activity as in the brain of a cocaine addict.

Less noticeable, but nonetheless occurring in the same manner, is the addiction to the stimulation caused by our environment—the Internet, our jobs, traffic, all of the constant input our brains receive relentlessly. As our baselines rise in an attempt to cope, we find ourselves needing more stimulation to feel normal. Without it, we feel depressed, anxious, and restless, and off we go to find more stimulation while at the same time complaining that we can't relax.

Food addiction

No discussion of addiction would be complete without exploring food addictions. Food addiction encompasses both substance and process addictions, since sugar is an addictive substance and the process of anticipation, eating compulsively to dull pain and fill emptiness, and feeling subsequent shame is in common with sex, gambling, and shopping.

Sugar is another natural substance whose properties have either been enhanced or the pleasure intensified through the creation of alternatives such as high fructose corn syrup or artificial sweeteners. As you have probably guessed, sugar stimulates the transmission of dopamine. Artificial sweeteners can be as much as three hundred times sweeter than regular sugar, which results in the brain raising the baseline to maintain the status quo. Sound familiar? This means that when you drink sugar-free sodas, you are setting up an additive process in your brain that will actually make you crave more sugar. Don't forget that we also get sugar from carbohydrates, as in bread and pasta, so you will crave them as much as cupcakes and soda.

DOCTOR, HOW CAN WE DIAGNOSE ADDICTION?

The *Diagnostic and Statistical Manual of Mental Disorders* (DSM) is used in the psychiatric and mental health community to define the criteria for any number of diagnoses, including substance dependence. The DSM-IV-TR uses a specific set of criteria for a diagnosis of addiction (see Appendix).

The DSM criterion specifies dependence as applicable to substances, such as cocaine or alcohol. How then can we apply it to behaviors such as sex, shopping, or gambling? Video games, texting, or chatting? It is simple: just substitute the word "behavior" where the DSM states "substance" and this is how we can make a diagnosis:

> Addiction is defined as a maladaptive pattern of **behavior** leading to clinically significant impairment or distress, as manifested by three (or more) of the following, occurring any time in the same 12-month period:
>
> 1. Tolerance, as defined by either of the following:
> (a) A need for markedly increased amounts of the **behavior** to achieve intoxication or

the desired effect (relief of pain, avoidance of intimacy, or engaging in pseudo-intimacy)

Or

(b) Markedly diminished effect with continued use of the same amount of the **behavior**. (A gambler going to the casino once a month, then once a week, and then daily and spending more and more time there and still feeling unsatisfied)

2. Withdrawal, as manifested by either of the following:

(a) The characteristic withdrawal syndrome for the **behavior** (symptoms of anxiety, depression, irritability)

Or

(b) The same (or closely related) **behavior** is done to relieve or avoid withdrawal symptoms (any behavior that provides the brain with stimulation can be substituted. The Caveman Brain will go for what is most readily available and make the new associations. A person may stop alcohol and find he is eating more or a smoker will quit and then stay at work half the night.)

3. The **behavior** is often done in larger amounts or over a longer period than intended. (A gamer may start out going online once or twice a week, then it becomes every night, then it goes on all night.)

4. There is a persistent desire or unsuccessful efforts to cut down or control the **behavior**. (The addict realizes there is a problem but is unable to stop.)

5. A great deal of time is spent in activities necessary to lead up to the **behavior**, do the **behavior**, or recover from its effects. (The addict may wait in line for the newest techno-toy, play with it for hours, and then be exhausted at work the next day.)

6. Important social, occupational, or recreational activities are given up or reduced because of the **behavior**. (The addict engages in the behavior during all free time and only socializes with others who share the addiction.)

7. The **behavior** is continued despite knowledge of having a persistent physical or psychological problem that is likely to have been caused or exacerbated by the **behavior** (for example, current gambling despite recognition of imminent financial disaster or continued working late every night despite recognition that one's children were failing in school).

The DSM uses the term "dependence" in a more medical context, but here we are using the term "addiction" to encompass the entire concept of obsessive, compulsive, out of control behavior done in spite of negative consequences to self or others.

It becomes clear that dependence, or addiction, is not just about a drug. It can be about anything to which we can become tolerant, causes us to experience withdrawal, or that is out of control, and from which we experience a whole range of negative consequences.

To be clear, this is about a specific behavior and only when that behavior meets the criteria for dependence or addiction. For instance, masturbation is usually a healthy and pleasurable activity that can enhance one's life; however, when a person thinks about masturbation while at work, goes to the restroom to masturbate, or stays on the computer until the wee hours of the morning masturbating to Internet pornography, then the behavior falls into the framework of addiction.

PART II
THE ADDICTIVE PROCESS:
DISCONNECTION

THE CHICKEN AND THE EGG CYCLE

Initially, stimulation causes the release of all those feel-good chemicals, like dopamine, but the addict brain eventually does not care what is causing the stimulation, it only wants it. The addict brain learns to make the association between a particular stimulator, be it pasta or procrastination, bread or beer, cigarettes or sex, and will put into motion any chain of events in order to be stimulated. If the regular stimulator is not available, it will find a replacement. That could be a different drug or a different activity—it is all stimulation to the brain (remember the DSM—the same or closely related behavior is done to relieve or avoid withdrawal symptoms). This is why so many people have multiple addictions and why even when an addict is not actively engaged with his or her drug or behavior of choice, he or she will seek stimulation in other ways, such as engaging in arguments or running late for appointments. The addict brain is always craving stimulation and is either thinking about it, preparing the way for it, receiving it, or recovering from its effects.

Keep in mind that an addict is always high. Personally, I am not an alcoholic, so when I'm at work and think about having a glass of wine at the end of the day, it is a passing thought and I may or may not actually follow through. I'm not obsessing about the day being over or compulsively looking at my watch. I don't rush out of my office and run over the dog in my effort to get to the wine cabinet. As I said, I'm not an alcoholic. If I was an alcoholic, I would be doing all of the above and I'd be getting high doing it. Looking at my watch and just thinking about taking that first gulp of wine would get me as high as a kid anticipating presents under the Christmas tree. As the time approached for actually getting that glass in hand, my dopamine transmitters would be firing at will.

I admit that I do engage in addictive behavior when I allow myself to feel stressed or overwhelmed. Rather than being present and focused on the task at hand, I want to get it finished so I can do something else and will be thinking about several things at once. In the end, I'm stressed, feel tired, and haven't done anything really well, nor have I been fully engaged with anyone with whom I've interacted.

For another example, a cocaine addict may go to work during the week but thoughts will slip in like "Friday night I'm going to party hearty!" or "I can't wait to hit the clubs this weekend!" The excitement builds until Friday, when there is the ritual of preparation, the dressing up, calling friends, going to the club, and finally scoring the cocaine. Then there is the actual using, which goes on through the night and may even continue throughout the weekend. By Monday morning, our guy is drained and empty, drags himself in to work (he has to keep his job so he can afford the cocaine), and slowly he recovers. But as bad as he feels, he's already thinking about the end of the week anticipating the next weekend binge. It's much like a song I remember from the '60s (yeah, I'm old) by the Easybeats—"Tonight, I'll lose my head, tonight, I'll spend my bread, tonight, I've got to get tonight. Monday I have Friday on my mind." Well, the '60s are when addiction really took off.

So which came first, the chicken or the egg? Addiction is not a linear process, it is circular.

What happens when someone tries to cut back or even quit? (Remember the description of the withdrawal syndrome—anxiety, depression, and irritability.) This person will begin creating reasons to use. *Airplane!,* a movie from the '80s that was a spoof on disaster airplane movies, featured a character in the flight tower (played by Lloyd Bridges) who was an unusually controlling fellow. He barked orders to everyone, including his wife, but when disaster struck, he started to unravel. At the first indication of something wrong, he took out a cigarette and said, "I guess I picked the wrong week to quit smoking." This theme continued with "I guess I picked the wrong week to quit drinking" as he took a big gulp from a flask to "I guess I picked the wrong week to quit amphetamines," and finally "I guess I picked the wrong week to quit sniffing glue." At this point, he was totally incapacitated and threw himself out the window.

What this illustrates is that addicts will use any excuse to continue getting high, even while realizing the negative effects of their addiction. If you know the movie, you will remember that the character played by Robert Stack was also right in the middle of the action, but he maintained a calm and steady demeanor. The same activating event elicited two extremely different reactions. Why? Each character had a choice about how much stress he was going to experience.

So now let's take this a step further. The example above is still linear in progression. What I am proposing is that the process is circular; the addict does not just respond to circumstances, he or she creates the circumstance that allows him or her to use.

An example of this is the woman who tells her husband that she will pay the electric bill. When she doesn't, her husband becomes angry and starts a fight. She then uses the fight to justify having a drink or escaping to the computer. Then she'll complain that it's not her fault, that her husband started the fight, that she was too busy with her job and the kids to pay the bill, and on and on and on. But she set up the circumstances. She knew that not paying the bill would infuriate her husband and provoke the fight. Whenever someone tells me of a circumstance that led to acting out or abusing a substance, my first question is, "What did you do to cause the event that made it okay for you to use?" (And no, I'm not letting the husband off the hook here. He is still responsible for his own behavior.)

One of the interesting things about this is that she did not consciously set up the fight . It was her addict brain that initiated the cycle that ultimately led to having an excuse for her addictive behavior. For now we will look at the addict brain as an entity in and of itself. Our eventual goal is to integrate the addict with the person, but it is helpful to understand how the brain works if we think of the addict brain like the wizard behind the curtain (remember *The Wizard of Oz?*)

How does this work with our process addictions? Procrastination is a good example. Here's a student who starts the semester taking five classes. She knows up front what books she will need, what the assignments are, when they are due, and when the exams will be held. She has the opportunity to structure her time to accomplish all the necessary tasks—reading, researching, studying, writing—within the deadlines and with a minimum of stress. So what happens? She buys her books a couple of weeks into the semester, she doesn't start researching her term paper until the week it is due, she stays up the night before the exam "pulling an all-nighter," and then tells herself and everyone else that she "works best under pressure." She will also complain that she has too much to do, that she had to cope with crises from every direction, and that her life is ruled by stress. And yet she created it all herself. Why? Because she got all those great feel-good brain chemicals racing around her head giving her all that stimulation she has come to need just to feel normal.

That's the real trap—that we need incredible amounts of stimulation to not feel bored, discontented, anxious, and generally jittery.

As a nation, we are not able to relax. We need incredibly high levels of stimulation all the time, from multiple directions. Personally, I find it difficult to do just one task at a time. If I am on the computer, I also have the television on. If I am talking on the phone, I'll be playing a computer game. I need to engage as many senses as possible to keep my mind focused, which is quite a conundrum. How does one focus when one is attending to several different stimuli?

It depends, of course, on which senses are engaged. When I am listening or talking on the phone, playing a simple game like solitaire engages my sense of sight but not my analytical processes, which are being used to converse. I am unable to play games that require analysis and still give full attention to the conversation. What many people do is not to pay full attention to those tasks that require it, but rather try to attend to several different things and then fill in the spaces as needed. Of course, this often does not work. This is why people get in so many car accidents. They drive along on autopilot, thinking that driving does not need their full attention, and so they use the same mental resources to attend to other activities, such as eating or talking on a cell phone. This works until something unexpected happens, such as another car cutting them off or a change in traffic patterns. The mind needs to switch from attending to one activity to another, and the time it takes to transfer attention is often not sufficient to respond to the new stimuli, resulting in an accident.

When we are involved in conversations without our full attention, we often miss vital pieces of information. The mind then has a tendency to make up information to fill in the blank, resulting in a lot of miscommunication. How many partners get into arguments over one person saying, "You never told me that we were scheduled to have dinner with the Smiths on Saturday!" and the other responding, "Yes I did, you just never listen to me!" And so it goes. Another opportunity to feel stressed and anxious and to create distance with someone, enabling the partners to go their separate ways and act out in whatever addictive way they choose. We're back to our fear of intimacy and Connection.

What is really scary is that we are teaching our children to be addicts. We are increasingly inundating them with information, activities, and technology to the point where they are completely unable to amuse themselves using only their own imaginations and resources. They expect constant external stimulation and we provide it. Look around at kids on the street. They have headphones providing aural stimulation, they are "texting" their friends on their cell phones, they are involved in constant after-school activities that require hurtling from one place to another, they are e-mailing and surfing the Internet on their computers, which are often a part of their cell phones now. They play video games and watch TV and play games on the TV. Their bedrooms overflow with toys and technology and they are unable to be alone with themselves for even five minutes to have an original thought or to contemplate their place in the universe.

You may say that they are creative in their ability to find solutions to computer games and you would be partially right, but a computer game is a program that was written within certain parameters, outside of which someone cannot go without re-writing the program. The ability to sit down with some basic materials, like popsicle sticks or clay, and create something unique is a joy that few children experience these days.

Those young people who strive to be creative in our society often turn to destructive activities to release their imaginations. It is in the void of a lack of guidance and direction where computer hackers and virus creators are produced. Children left on their own will give rein to their need to create and also to feel in control.

LOCUS OF CONTROL or THE FEAR FACTOR

The Serenity Prayer
> God, grant me the serenity to accept the things I cannot change,
> The courage to change the things I can, and
> The wisdom to know the difference.

This prayer is said daily by millions of recovering addicts the world over, and I recommend it to everyone as a guide to life and relationships. What does it mean? In brief, the things I cannot change are everything outside of me. The things I can change are me—my thinking, feelings, and behavior.

Addiction is about control and the lack of it. We think we are in control when we are not. We try to control what we cannot—external factors, such as other people or situations—and don't control what we can—internal factors, which are our own thoughts, feelings, and behaviors. (Lloyd Bridges and Robert Stack in *Airplane!* could not control the external situation, but they could each control their internal response to it.)

Control is about feeling safe. It goes back to the baby that did not get its needs met, that was not cared for or shown love, and took in the message that there must be something wrong with it and the world is not a safe place. Fear is at the root of all our problems, and anger is the tip of the iceberg of fear. If I am angry, it is because I really fear something. You don't believe this? It can be difficult, but let's look at it.

Cognitive-behavior theory states that the way we think leads to how we feel. If we can change our thinking, we can change, or control, our feelings, like anger.

Our fears are existential—they all come down to a few basic thoughts: I am worthless, I am unlovable, I will always be abandoned, and I'm not good enough. The most basic fear is that I will be alone.

We are social beings and need to belong to a group—family, religion, culture, race, school, or community. The list is endless. Our need to belong to and be accepted by our groups is the driving force behind all of our behavior. Just like addiction, our fear of being excluded from our group can lead us to betray our values and withdraw from our intimate attachments. Cults are the extreme manifestation of this in that they offer acceptance to the group with the condition that the member adheres only to that group and forsakes all others. Conversely, a true awareness of the Connectedness of all living things and the embracing of that Connection allows a person to never fear being alone and to always feel a belonging to the Universe, even beyond death. Everything can be reduced to this most primal fear, which governs our feelings and behavior. Death, of course, is often feared as the ultimate aloneness, so our fear of death governs a considerable portion of our behavior. Not convinced? Let's look at some examples.

When asked what thoughts make us angry, we will often say, "Nothing, I just got angry," but that is not really true. It is because the thought is so habitual that we are not aware of it. For instance, if a car cuts me off in traffic, I get angry. At the time, I don't analyze what I am thinking, I just get angry. But what is the underlying thought? I might tell myself that the driver almost caused an accident (fear of death) or did not respect me (fear of worthlessness or not being good enough, which means that no one will love me and I will be alone).

If my husband criticizes my cooking, I may respond angrily as a result of thinking, "I'm not good enough and he will leave me (fear of abandonment)." Or I may say to myself, "He is not the man of my dreams and we will not make it (fear of being alone)."

It is not always evident when we think in this manner. These thoughts are usually part of an ingrained pattern and therefore unconscious, but when you can slow down the process, the basic fears emerge and a common theme will become apparent. Furthermore, the thoughts are usually not rational. Albert Ellis, the creator of Rational Emotive Behavior Therapy (one of the cognitive-behavioral theories), developed the idea that we are at the mercy of our irrational thoughts and that when we can identify and change those thoughts, we can change our feelings. It is the irrational idea of not being good enough or of always being abandoned that drives our feelings and behavior. These irrational thoughts usually develop in childhood and become so ingrained in our psyche that we are unaware of their power over us.

In my years as a therapist, I have very often heard variations of the same history. A child comes home from school with a B and the parent berates her for not getting an A. When the child does get an A, it goes unremarked. The parent no doubt believes the right message is being conveyed, that the child should work hard to always get A's in order to be successful in life. In reality, the child takes in the message that she is "not good enough" and will never be good enough. She may take either of two roads: keep working hard trying to get affirmation and fill the need to be good enough or give up even trying because she does not believe anything will ever be good enough. The first road will lead to compulsive working and striving for success as defined by money and praise (there's our work addict) and the second will look for pain relievers to escape the belief of her own inferiority (drugs, shopping, gambling, food, etc.).

Children will take in messages in other ways as well. There is a paradox at work here. Children believe that they are the center of the universe and have control over everything, yet they inherently know that they are incapable of handling that power, so they are always engaged in struggles with authority so that they can be reassured that someone else is really in control. When they don't get that reassurance, they push the envelope until they do. Some don't stop until they end up in prison, where they finally feel safe because a strict authority is now in control.

Most children do feel some sense of safety with their parents, but parents aren't always aware of the workings of a child's mind. If the parents get divorced, for instance, a child is likely to believe that it is his fault and will grow up with that sense of self-blame—"There is something wrong with me, I'm not good enough, I'm not important." Just like the baby in the wet diapers, a child who is ignored will believe it must be something about him, not understanding that maybe Mom and Dad had to work two jobs just to pay the mortgage and buy groceries. When the child becomes an adult, he may cognitively understand that, but the inner child will still play that message of not being important or good enough into adult relationships. The power to feel important has an external locus of control as the adult child looks for that reassurance in other relationships.

Parents inherently have control over their children, so they have tremendous power to shape their lives through these messages, often unspoken and misunderstood. As children become adults, however, they can begin to understand that they can control their own messages and change those messages received in childhood. In other words, they can move the control from external to internal.

I remember an episode from the 1990s show *Northern Exposure*, about a woman who was competing in a wheelchair race. While she measured her success against the other competitors, she experienced pain in her arm that seemed to have no cause. Ed, the shaman-in-training, was able to discover her battle with the character "External Validation" and defeat him. The woman began measuring her success only in relation to her own personal best and the pain in her arm vanished.

Slowing down the process that leads to anger or depression can help us identify the patterns to our irrational thoughts and we can begin to see how a fear of abandonment or of being alone drives our feelings and behavior. If I approach every new relationship with the expectation that I will be abandoned, then sooner or later I will look for signs that the other person is getting ready to leave me. I will be jealous and insecure, possessive and anxious. I will press for constant reassurances, although they will never be enough. (This is important, because trying to get the external validation that I am "good enough" only gives the power and control to the other person. Since the belief is within me, nothing anyone says or does will ever be "enough" for me.) I will eventually pick fights and provoke the very thing that I fear in either a conscious or unconscious desire to have it happen and end the tension. You probably know people who behave this way. You may even be one.

What does this have to do with addiction? Well, a couple of things actually. First, stress is addictive, so the stress of wondering when the abandonment will occur keeps the stimulation levels high. If the stimulation levels begin to decrease, the addict brain will begin craving excitement and create new situations that will produce stress. So if I begin to allow myself to believe that my new partner may actually love me and want to be with me, that he will not abandon me and that I am a worthwhile person, then my addict brain will find a reason to doubt again. He doesn't call me one night, he wants to go out with some friends, he didn't bring me flowers, and the list goes on. I tell myself that he will leave me, my stress rises, and my addict brain gets its fix. The subsequent fighting, crying, and recriminations will also provide the stimulation my brain is looking for. There may also be attempts from my honey to prove to me that he does care about me, so the extra attention, great sex, and intense conversations also provide more grist for my addict mill. How many times have you heard people say that they fight just so they can make up? It is the constant turbulence that keeps the arousal levels elevated. Without the fighting and making up, life seems boring and bland.

The other part of this addictive angle is that we use drugs and addictive activities to escape from pain, and the existential agony of abandonment and loneliness is the greatest pain there is. Fighting and worrying and creating drama keep the brain occupied and allow avoidance of pain. Constant avoidance of pain through one medium, be it drugs, work, gambling, sex, shopping, or food, leads to addiction. Then the addictive acting out causes more pain in the form of recognition of how one's life is out of control and causing negative consequences to self or others, but the addict has only the one way to deal with pain, which is more acting out, so the cycle continues.

Understanding the concept of "locus of control" is integral to recovery from addiction.

"Locus of control" relates to where the control is located—or where is the power. It is either external or internal, and we can take it or give it away. External controllers are the weather, the traffic, our bosses, law enforcement, and the IRS. These are all things that we feel are in control of our lives, and the more we feel controlled by them, the unhappier we are likely to be. It's raining, so my weekend is ruined. The traffic is heavier all the time, so I am more likely to be late. My boss wants me to work harder, take more responsibility, doesn't like me, harasses me, so I feel frustrated and hate going to work in the morning. The cops don't see the guy who almost hit me, lawyers are all crooked, and no one likes paying taxes. All of these are the thoughts that lead to feelings of anger and frustration and are rooted in general feelings of powerlessness.

We give away our power when we say "She made me angry" or "That makes me miserable." By giving away our power in this manner, we are really saying "I want to be angry but I don't want to take responsibility for it." There is a childish aspect to this, isn't there? Can't you just see the little child stamping her foot, claiming, "You're making me miserable and want me to be unhappy!"

The truth is, no one can "make" us have any particular feelings. They can say or do something (the activating event), but we then choose how to feel because of it. Addicts are more likely to choose to be angry, hurt, or frustrated than otherwise, because it gives them an excuse to do their drugs or addictive behavior. Some people think that their spouse wants to make them angry for some perverted purpose of their own, but then why are they with that person? We pick and choose what makes us angry and what makes us happy and then choose whether or not to take credit for it. We all have hidden agendas, and the addict's agenda is always "How can I justify my addictive behavior?" Remember my question, "What are you doing to cause this situation?"

In looking for the underlying sources of pain, fear, and emptiness, I have found useful another cognitive-behavioral theory called **transactional analysis** (TA). It is based on how we communicate with others and why. A *transaction* is a completed communication. I ask you to go for a ride with me and you say yes, I'd love to, and off we go. Transactions can be open and straightforward, such as "Please pass the salt," which means I want the salt, or ulterior, such as "Are you going to eat those fries?" meaning "I want your fries but I'm trying to be polite" or "What's your sign, do you come here often?" which means "Do we have anything at all in common because I want to have sex with you!" Some ulterior transactions are readily understood, such as the ones above. Others can be misunderstood and lead to miscommunication, arguments, and distancing or lack of intimacy.

TA identifies three ego states from which we communicate:
– Parent
– Adult
– Child

When Debbie says to her husband, "The dog needs a bath," and he replies, "Yes, I noticed he rolled in something dead," they are communicating Adult to Adult. There are no power plays, no heavy emotional overtones. If she communicates from her Parent Ego State to his Child Ego State, she might say "What's wrong with you? Can't you smell that dog? Why haven't you given him a bath?" Her husband has a choice, though, from which Ego State he can respond. He might reply from his Adult Ego State, "Yes, dear, I did notice a bad odor and will wash the dog in half an hour." Or he might reply from his Child Ego State, saying, "Why are you always yelling at me? I can't do everything around here!" The former equalizes the relationship between them, opening the way for intimacy. By choosing to not reply defensively, he is in effect telling her that he recognizes her concern and will attend to the specific problem. Unless she has an ulterior motive of provoking a fight or of maintaining a controlling posture, they will move on from that situation without further discord.

The latter response is more likely to provoke further conflict and lead to some eventual confirmation for Debbie that she always has to do everything, that he is just a big spoiled child, that she is superior.

This thinking keeps their relationship unequal and therefore Disconnected, or lacking true intimacy. When people are not interacting as equals and when one person takes a superior position, they cannot be intimate and Connected. We see these patterns everywhere in relationships—one person taking a parental role to the other's child role. Both parties express unhappiness with the condition but seem unable to change it. Both will blame the other, but each will behave in a manner to maintain it. Why do people do this, especially when their Enlightened Brain is saying "I want to be equal to you, I want to be Connected and intimate?"

TA says that we develop "Life Scripts" in our early years. These scripts are imparted either verbally or non-verbally, and the latter are more powerful. We learn what we see—from our parents, our peers, our culture, and our religions. Once we have our scripts, we communicate in ways that validate them. We run the same play over and over again. It is only when we become aware of the script that we can make a decision to change it, and change is seldom easy. In other words, the script gets conditioned into the limbic system, but it can be changed when the Enlightened Brain becomes aware of it.

One example of a life script that has little emotional content but demonstrates the power of mindless influence on learning comes from an old *Reader's Digest* story. It tells of a young woman, newly married, who was cooking a roast for her husband. He was in the kitchen with her, watching her every move lovingly when he noticed that she cut the ends off the roast before putting it in the pan. He asked her what the purpose of this was and she replied that it was what her mother had always done. Intrigued, he called her mother and asked her about this interesting cooking ritual, and the mother replied that it was what her mother had always done. Fully engaged in tracking down the origins of this odd behavior, the husband called his wife's grandmother and asked her why she always cut the ends off the roast, and the grandmother replied "When I was first married, we only had one roasting pan and it was too small for the roast, so I had to cut the ends off to make it fit."

This is how life scripts get started, and we can see how much of our behavior and much of the world's behavior is based on some ancient script that had a purpose at one time but now has become a tradition with no practical basis and may even be self-defeating. Debbie, in the stinky dog example, may have absorbed the message from her life script that women are in charge and that men are just big boys who need to be told what to do. Or she may believe that if she does not rule her house with a firm hand, she will be a failure as a wife. Irrational thoughts or outmoded scripts, they all have the same effect: Disconnection and lack of intimacy.

A person communicating from a Parent Ego State is attempting to control the other, while a person communicating from a Child Ego State is relinquishing control. This external locus of control leads to feeling out of control, which leads to doing more of the behavior to take control, which leads to turning to an addictive behavior that gives the illusion of control, which leads to life being completely out of control!

All external control is an illusion. True control only lies in our own minds. More specifically, it lies in the pre-frontal cortex—the Enlightened Brain. We have the power to change our irrational thoughts and life scripts and take responsibility for our feelings and behavior. Now, do we want to?

Victor Frankl, an existentialist and the originator of logotherapy, was interred in a concentration camp in World War II. He suffered all of the horrors of this experience, but he came through it with a sense of internal power that was untouched by his captors. He was able to believe that the Nazis could not touch his mind, whatever they did to his body and to those around him. He developed the concept that we all need to find meaning in life and that we do this through our experiences. We have a choice with each experience—to be passive with it or to find the meaning in it. This concept is not about predetermination or that our lives are predestined and we just have to accept them. It is about actively creating our own meaning from our own experiences.

When I work with addicts seeking recovery, I ask them to search for the meaning in life and to make a conscious decision about *what* they want their lives to mean. What stamp do they want to make on the world? How can they leave the world a better place? How can they make a positive difference in even one person's life?

Changing thoughts, feelings, and behavior in order to live a more Connected life is not for the faint hearted. It is risky and takes great courage. To open oneself up to all of those existential bogeys—abandonment, rejection, isolation—to take that risk requires an awesome leap onto the unknown plane of true Connection and intimacy. It truly rocks our world.

Why is intimacy and Connection so frightening? That's easy: if we are truly intimate and Connected, then we are completely exposed to another person. Exposure means that the other person will see and know our innermost selves, including all our shameful secrets, so what could happen then? The other person will be disgusted, repulsed, or even derisive, which will lead to—you know the answer to this one—being rejected, abandoned, and alone!

How do we get past this? How do we attain true intimacy and Connection? By letting go of our shame. Not so easy, but just think of a time when you revealed something shameful to another person only to find that they had a similar secret or they responded in a warm and compassionate manner. Maybe you revealed a secret and in the telling realized that it really wasn't so bad. Secrets and shame tend to fester and grow in the dark but will wither and dry and blow away when exposed to the light of revelation.

Alcoholics Anonymous, the original self-help group for addicts helping addicts, has a tradition of each person beginning their sharing with the introduction "Hi, I'm Jon, and I'm an alcoholic/addict." The rest of the members in the room respond with "Hi, Jon." The purpose of this is threefold. First, it is an affirmation of one's status as an addict, a way of breaking through denial and "keeping it green" as they say. Each time an addict makes that admission, he or she is saying "I am not trying to pretend that I'm not an addict, I'm not trying to fool myself or you."

Next, it is a revelation of something that has been shameful, has been a secret. Addicts may spend years in shame and secrecy, which of course is part of the denial. By proclaiming "I am an addict," they are revealing this shameful secret in a manner that rejects the shame and destroys the secrecy, as well as implies an expectation of trust and acceptance from the receiving audience. The addict is saying "I am open. This is who I am, for better or worse. I am worthy of your respect and acceptance. I trust that you will not reject me."

Finally, the response from the fellowship is the acknowledgment of the offering of trust and affirmation: "Yes, we accept you, we are here for you, your secret is not shameful to us, we honor you for your willingness to be here with us."

Very few people live their lives with this kind of openness, and quite often those that do are recovering addicts. Addiction strips away everything from a person—possessions, job, relationships, and self-respect. The First Step from AA says "We admit we are powerless," meaning that the addict is powerless over the addiction and that powerlessness is what an individual must finally face to begin a new life of recovery, which is one of Connection with a higher power and subsequent intimacy with other individuals and all living beings.

This is another paradox of addiction, which the Serenity Prayer defines. We are powerless over everything external and only become truly powerful when we recognize this and control only ourselves. Possessions *represent* power, money *represents* power, relationships *represent* power, but they are all illusions because they are external and we cannot truly control anything external, only our internal beliefs about ourselves.

This is why intimacy is so intimidating and difficult. We must lose the idea that we are in control, including the idea that we can control what another person thinks or feels about us by choosing what we reveal to them. We must take the risk of revealing our most shameful secrets to another person and hope that we will be loved and accepted regardless. So now ask yourself, "With whom am I truly intimate?"

THE TECHNOLOGY DRUG or I WANT WHAT I WANT WHEN I WANT IT

Every generation has had its innovative technology, its way of enhancing the stimulation provided by our "toys," which gets people scrambling to accommodate and keep up (iPhone, anyone?)

When automobiles began to catch on, a substantial number of people jumped in and took off. Twenty-five miles an hour, "Whooo hoooo!" A thirst for speed developed. The old timers looked on with disdain and made denigrating remarks about people tearing up the countryside and frightening the horses, but cars caught on and became faster and sleeker to the point where guys here in Miami are buying Ferraris, not because they have any hope of driving them 150 miles an hour on our congested highways, but because they represent status and power and hope that someday they will wake up to empty streets and be able to really let loose. Just sitting behind the wheel on Ocean Drive and revving the engine shoots their adrenaline level up way above base line. Sound familiar?

One of my favorite books of all times, *The Wind in the Willows* by Kenneth Grahame, has a character by the name of Toad who is quite wealthy and becomes addicted to motorcars. This book was written in 1908, when automobiles were just coming on the scene, and the transformation of Toad from an animal who already had an addictive personality but was kept in check by the limits of the technology of the day into a ravening speed-demon who blew through his inheritance and ended up in prison is a story that illustrates every aspect of addiction. His friends Badger, Rat, and Mole even did an intervention on him!

Cars, trains, and planes are all ways to go faster, get there sooner, and do more in a shorter period of time. Every invention that is touted as being a time saver that will allow us more leisure time has proven to do the reverse. The housewife with the electric dishwasher and frozen dinners in the 1950s suddenly had the time to go outside the home to work to pay for the second car she needed to drive to work and to drive the kids to the myriad of activities they now did because they had to keep busy. Every efficiency tool at work only leads to more job duties.

As a nation, we revere hard work and have the utmost contempt for slackers. Relaxation is a myth. Our idea of relaxing is to fill our time with sports, games, and *doing*. We talk about taking off a week and *doing nothing*, but in reality that lasts an hour, an afternoon, maybe even a day, and then the restlessness begins. We jump up and look for something to do. We find chores, we make phone calls, we pace, we jump in the car and go shopping, go to the movies, go *somewhere* to escape the emptiness of nothing.

More recently, we don't have to leave home to "do something." Our computers and Blackberries allow us to be doing something nonstop. What's more, we don't need to physically interact with anyone. We can connect with the world without touching another living being. This inability to do nothing, in addiction language, is called *withdrawal.* As our drugs wear off and we begin craving more, we experience the withdrawal symptoms common to all addictions—anxiety, restlessness, and depression.

Have you ever heard a smoker say that cigarettes calm him down, that he needs a cigarette to calm him? How can this be when nicotine is actually a central nervous system stimulant? It is because after a smoker puts out a cigarette, the process of craving begins. The addict wants his fix. So over a period of time, minutes or maybe hours, the craving builds to the point where the smoker is withdrawing from the drug and begins to suffer the anxiety and restlessness. So he lights up and *whammo!* He calms down.

I remember in the '70s technology brought us video games. I personally fed innumerable quarters into a Space Invaders game machine in the bar where I was working. Cigarettes have been my only addiction, but I came close with that one. Other bar patrons were not so moderate, and I remember some folks spending hours on end at that machine. The good news was that they became so good at the game they did not have to spend much money. The bad news was that they just stood there staring at the screen, oblivious to the world. They did not interact with anyone in the room and certainly were not interacting with whoever might have been waiting at home for them. Of course, maybe that was the problem: no one was waiting.

More video game machines were invented to feed the need for new challenges, and then the '90s ushered in widespread use of the Internet and a whole new level of addiction took hold of the nation. Addictive behaviors that formerly took a certain amount of time and energy, thereby keeping them under some control, now became limitless and overwhelming (the effects were intensified). Where shopping used to involve getting into the car and going to the mall, now it only requires turning on the computer and clicking on an ad. You can even store your information so you don't need to spend valuable time typing in your address or credit card number. An addict can strip her savings and max out her credit cards in a matter of days or even hours with online purchases. No longer is it necessary to drive all the way to a store and walk that tedious length of the parking lot. Just a couple of clicks and every mall in the world is in front of her. Of course, there is always that delightful face-to-face interaction with the friendly UPS delivery person with whom she is on a first name basis. Who said this was a solitary activity?

Where gambling used to require going to the track or the casino, now there are innumerable gambling web sites where several games can be played at the same time. Here in south Florida, as in other parts of the country, we hear a lot about gambling. The almost defunct race dog tracks have managed to hang on by offering other gambling activities, such as slot machines and simulcast betting on horse races around the country. Jai alai, a game brought with the Latin American immigrants, has lost popularity in recent years but is hanging on with poker and simulcast betting. It is not uncommon to enter a jai alai fronton or dog track and find the stands almost empty of spectators, but there will be numerous people behind the counters taking bets from gamblers who can make wagers on games and races anywhere in the country.

We also have the Indian Reservation, which has long had gambling in its casino out in the Everglades. More recently, the Hard Rock Casino opened, and the gaming tables are filled morning, noon, and night. Giant billboards have now sprung up advertising help for those with gambling problems as evidence of this surge in escapism that is enticing thousands. Casinos are not kept rich by the casual patron out for a night of fun. It is the addicts that pour their money onto the tables until their lives are in ruins with relationships lost, bank accounts emptied, and self-esteem in tatters. All that is left is the craving to go back one more time, the dream that the next throw of the dice will be the big win. The trap, as with all addictive behavior, is that there is never enough.

And of course, there's pornography.

Internet porn has helped to create millions of new addicts. There are millions of porn sites, accessible to all. You can get what you want, when you want it. As the brain becomes inured to the multitude of images of women and men having intercourse or oral sex, it seeks for more stimulation in the form of other types of sexual behavior, from multiple partners to fetishistic behavior to sado-masochism to any of the hundreds of sexual variations available at the click of a mouse. Let me say here that I am not suggesting that any particular behavior is wrong or immoral if it is between consenting adults. This is not about values or religion or restrictions on sexual expression. It is about sexual behavior that is obsessive, compulsive, out of control, and done in spite of negative consequences to self and others.

So when someone is on the Internet looking at porn while at work or school, knowing that he could be caught and fired or expelled, that is addictive. A father who spends time looking at porn sites rather than helping his kids with their homework is an addict. A husband who masturbates to porn rather than making love with his wife is an addict. A woman who is online flirtatiously chatting to anonymous men instead of spending quality time with her husband and children is an addict. Most importantly, the person who knows, on some level, that the behavior is causing a Disconnect and lack of intimacy and who sooner or later experiences shame and remorse is an addict.

Are women as addicted as men, you ask? Most porn addicts are men, simply because men's brains are more tuned in to visual cues for sex than women's brains. Men's brains are also biologically programmed to work in a more narrowly focused way than women—they are more goal-directed from those caveman days when they had to devise strategies and carry out plans to hunt down game. Women can certainly become addicted to any array of behaviors, but when it comes to the Internet, a woman will more likely become addicted to chatting and forming online relationships than to pornographic images.

The Internet has spawned many other addictions as well. Kids are now on social networking sites such as Facebook or Twitter, creating their personal web pages and building lists of friends to talk with online rather than going to the local soda shop (I'm dating myself) and talking face to face with another person. They text and type endlessly as they lose all sense of governance or inhibitory control. Whatever pops into their heads is immediately broadcast to the world, where all the other young addicts are immediately stimulated. Again there is this process of needing more to get the same effect. More friends on Facebook, more "Tweets" and texts from more people, more stimulation.

There is also a vast network of "gamers," people who engage in playing games online with others from around the world. They will spend hours playing in the virtual world rather than interacting with people in the real one. Sites such as Second Life and World of

Warcraft allow people to create whole other identities, or avatars, with which to interact with other avatars, so not only are the interactions a step removed in that they are not occurring in physical proximity, they are not even occurring between two real people. Talk about a lack of intimacy!

As the players become more immersed in who they want to be, not who they are, they become increasingly fearful of intimacy (here we go again!), of not being accepted as they are, of being rejected, unloved, and ultimately alone. And so the addictive cycle is magnified.

Thus this instant gratification that our American way of life provides us is a fundamental aspect of the creation of our addictions. We flood our brains with dopamine with every new form of stimulation and begin the cycle of tolerance and craving that define addiction. Why do we care? Because no win, no purchase, no orgasm, and no high will ever be enough to still the cravings or fill the emptiness.

THE CONNECTION CONNECTION or THE GREAT DISCONNECT

No man is an island
> No man is an island entire of itself; every man
> is a piece of the continent, a part of the main;
> if a clod be washed away by the sea, Europe
> is the less, as well as if a promontory were, as
> well as any manner of thy friends or of thine
> own were; any man's death diminishes me,
> because I am involved in mankind.
> And therefore never send to know for whom
> the bell tolls; it tolls for thee.
> > John Donne

Human beings are social animals. We live and work in communities; we rely on each other to meet our needs, from the most basic of shelter and food to the higher social, love, and affirmation needs.

John Donne's poem is a confirmation that we are each a part of something greater than ourselves, greater than our social group, greater than our country, greater than the world.

If you doubt this, then just choose which of the following statements is true:

1. I am the greatest power in the universe
2. I am not the greatest power in the universe.

God, the Higher Power, the Force, the Universe, the Light, the Tree of Life—whatever you prefer to call it—is a synergy. The whole is greater than the sum of the parts. We are all a part of God (the term used here for simplicity but don't be surprised when I use others, and feel free to substitute your own preference) and God is greater than everything. We are like cells within an organism, living entities that make up something so vast and complex we cannot even begin to comprehend its scope, and yet we have awareness of our lives and awareness of our Connection within the whole.

This theme has been prevalent throughout history in religion, philosophy, and political ideation. It is at the heart of our media culture in the *Stars Wars* trilogies and, more recently, *Avatar.* These movies were enormously successful, in large part because this theme of a unifying Force or Tree of Life truly resonates within all of us. What seems to be missing for many, however, is the conscious awareness of what *Star Wars* and *Avatar* touch within us. Our addictive brains are so focused on the high from the stunning visual special effects and technology that we come away from the experience wanting more of that rather than taking time to fully contemplate what it means to our real lives to be a part of the Force or the Tree of Life. It is there, just under the surface of our awareness, but we do not allow ourselves to be caught up in it, to feel it and appreciate it, to live it, preferring instead the pseudo-intimacy of sharing the 3-D and Blu-Ray experience. Yet without the theme of Connection, none of these movies would have the same impact. They would just be the next level of cinematic wizardry that would quickly be forgotten as we all move on to the next high. Our souls recognize and yearn for the Connection depicted in these great works; now we just need to really acknowledge what they mean to our spiritual lives.

Human Connection is a driving factor in every aspect of our existence. We identify with a particular family, culture, religion, and country. We join clubs and social groups. Unfortunately, those in society lacking other group affiliations because of some fear or inability to fit in or be accepted are easily led to join gangs or cults.

It is the fear of being excluded or exiled from our group or tribe that is the motivator for all of our behavior. We fear being alone. This fear will even overrule our personal beliefs and ethics.

An extreme example of this is the cultural ritual that is called genital mutilation, which is the practice of removing the clitoris and labia of young girls and sewing the vaginal opening almost completely shut. This has existed in half of Africa and parts of Asia and the Middle East for thousands of years. It is a practice that is no less than torture for the girls on whom it is performed and serves no purpose other than the perpetuation of a tradition begun centuries ago to subjugate women, and yet it continues because any girl or mother of a girl who wishes to escape this practice will be exiled from her family and community.

Various cults, like the infamous Branch Davidians or the People's Temple that Jim Jones founded, collect members through their welcoming acceptance of troubled outcasts and those looking for a life that they cannot find in their real existence. They maintain members' allegiance through peer pressure and threat of exile. The pain of Disconnection from the cult outweighs all physical pain, all ethical compromise, and all other losses. The irony is that these groups insist on Disconnection from the rest of the world. Any association with a friend, family member, or other person who is not part of the chosen group is forbidden. Any knowledge other than what the group imparts is also forbidden. In essence, the group becomes Disconnected from the rest of the world, with all of the spiritual deadening that entails. This is the way in which the group controls its members—it first accepts them, then isolates them, then threatens exclusion if they are not compliant.

Sometimes, however, contrary behavior exists among members of exclusionist groups, which seems to indicate that the members do want to reach out and Connect. I remember a time when I was sitting at an outdoor café in Key West watching the endless stream of cars and people go by. A car with four young people stopped right in front of the restaurant for a few minutes as they waited for a light. The car was a convertible and the radio was on full blast, playing what I and probably most of the other tourists considered extremely obnoxious noise. I observed these kids sitting silent, staring straight ahead, their almost blank expressions hinting at disdain and rebellious arrogance. Everything about them seemed designed to push the world away, and yet there was that music we were all sharing, albeit unwillingly. It made me think of times when I have been driving along in my car, carefree, listening to Van Morrison's "Brown-eyed Girl," singing along at the top of my lungs. At those times, I want to open the window and share it with everyone on the road. I want to see their hands start tapping; see them smile, maybe even sing along. I want to Connect.

As I sat watching these adolescents in search of identity (as all adolescents are, and yes, I consider many teens as part of an exclusionist group), I wondered if this was their way of unconsciously trying to Connect. What would happen if I gave some indication that I enjoyed their music? Would I see a hint of a smile? Would we experience one of those moments out of time and place when souls touch?

Another time, when my husband and I were driving north on I-95, that infamous highway of interminable traffic jams, toward Fort Lauderdale, all traffic came to a stop next to the airport and we resigned ourselves to an indefinite wait. As we looked across three lanes of traffic toward the airport runway, we noticed a jet preparing for take-off. Suddenly we both realized that it was the Concorde, now defunct, but then on one of its last insanely fast trips across the Pond. We were entranced as we watched it taxi, turn, rev its engines, blast away from us at an impossible speed, and then lift into the clouds. We let out our breaths and began looking around at the other cars. As we made eye contact and smiled at the other drivers, we all shared a Connection that existed only in that moment but was more powerful than that jet. We would never know each other, never knowingly see each other again, but we had shared that one experience and made that Connection. As the traffic moved on, we felt a lightness of spirit that had not been there at the start of our ride, but whenever I remember that moment, I feel it again and smile.

Connection is a driving force within all of us. Freud identified sex and death as the two unconscious forces that drive all human behavior, but both of those are really about Connection and the fear of losing it. Sex can be an expression of true love and intimacy or a pseudo-intimate act by two people wanting to Connect but afraid of the loss of control. Death is about connecting with God, with loved ones who have already passed on, or about Connection with the Universe. Most religions and spiritual beliefs have some explanation of life after death, so it makes sense that there are Connections or re-Connections to be made when we die.

For many of us, though, we fear death for ourselves for the loss of what we have here on earth, and we fear it for our loved ones as the end of our Connection with them. However you view it, Freud was still on to something when he developed this theory to explain how we think and why we behave as we do.

Jesus, whether you believe he was the son of God, a prophet, or simply a teacher, spent his life trying to promote the message of love and forgiveness. These concepts—love your neighbor (neighbors being everyone in the world) and forgive your enemies (an enemy being anyone who has ever inspired hatred, fleeting or perpetual, from guy who cut you off in traffic to Adolf Hitler)—encompass Connection. It is difficult, if not impossible for some, to feel a Connection to someone utterly hateful, someone like a serial killer, brutal dictator, child molester, or the neighbor who poisoned your dog, and yet that is what Jesus, Gandhi, the Dalai Lama, and other teachers of peace would have us do.

There is a saying, "There but for the grace of God go I." We usually say this when we see someone less fortunate than ourselves, someone with a disability or a victim of an accident or illness, and yet it is just as applicable when we contemplate those who are able to perpetrate evil acts that harm others. What gene, what chemical imbalance, what set of life circumstances led them to that place where they believe that their actions are justified, where they can actually feel satisfaction or even joy in someone else's suffering?

Selfish or selfless—which is which?

Whatever the cause, the ability to perpetrate suffering and harm on another being comes from being Disconnected. When I am Connected and aware of my Connection to all life, I am unable to cause harm because I feel the pain I am causing. There is no altruism, no lack of selfishness in doing good instead of harm. It is, in fact, selfish to help others and want to bring pleasure to others. Think about it—when you give a gift, when you make someone smile, or when you say something kind, don't you feel good? Don't you smile? When you help someone in trouble, when you donate to a cause, when you answer a call from a friend in the middle of the night, maybe you are put out or aggravated, but don't you do it because not to do it would cause you pain and discomfort? Maybe you do uncomfortable acts of goodness because you enjoy the rewards of praise and commendation from others. Maybe you do it because you feel empathy for the other person. There are degrees of Connection.

This brings to mind the parent who disciplines the child and says, "This hurts me more than it hurts you!" The parent is feeling the child's suffering not just from the punishment imposed, but from the child's resentment at being punished and/or the shame that he let his parents down and the Disconnect the child is feeling from the parent. The parent is attempting to say "We are still Connected, I am feeling this with you, and it is a measure of the importance of teaching you a lesson that I have to cause us both this pain, but I am with you in it." It is seldom, of course, that the child gets this until he has become a parent himself.

I don't mean to take away any of the goodness of the acts of kindness and generosity performed by anyone.

I am emphasizing that these can be acts committed out of Connection and that we cannot so easily separate the self from others. Furthermore, contrary to popular belief in America, there is nothing wrong with being selfish! The harm comes from placing oneself above others to their detriment. Causing pain without feeling that pain is about Disconnection. Profit at others' expense is about Disconnection. Putting another down in order to feel good about oneself is about Disconnection. Doing acts of kindness to control others' perception of us is about Disconnection. Disconnection is about separation of self from life and is the cause of all evil, all unhappiness, and all destruction.

How does this relate to addiction?

- Connection to others is Connection to the Universe.
- Intimacy is the experiencing of Connection.
- Addiction is a barrier to intimacy.

Addiction is about filling an emptiness within us, filling a hole in our souls that is the result of not feeling Connected. There are many paradoxes in addiction and this is one: that in trying to fill that emptiness, that hole, with addictive behavior cannot work, ever. No amount of drugs, sex, money, or accolades will ever be enough to feel good enough, important enough, or loved enough. Only through giving, through an outpouring of love and compassion, can we fill the hole and heal the emptiness. The emptiness comes from the lack of Connection and focus on self to the exclusion of others.

Have you ever noticed that when you are fully involved in some activity, like playing a sport or working on a project, you are completely unaware of yourself? You may have an aching back or are worried about paying the light bill, but in those moments that you are focused on the activity, you are not conscious of the pain and worry. This is even more apparent when you are focused on another person, when you leave the world in your own head to enter their world. By sending your energy outwards on a stream of compassion and caring, your own troubles cease to exist for a time.

Addiction is about taking in something to try to escape from pain and worry, but it is temporary and does not heal the soul or fill the void. Donuts and alcohol, sex and drugs, work and shopping—they are all temporary bandages that, in blocking those feelings we don't want, end up blocking those we do. Connection is healing and filling and allows the full range of human experience.

I read a short story several years ago—I think it was in *Reader's Digest*—that illustrates Connection through a higher power. The story includes Jesus, but you may substitute Gandhi or Buddha or any name you wish. It goes like this:

A man was driving his car through a snowstorm one night. The road was dark and the world was only a swirling cloud of snow through which he could not see even through his headlights. Suddenly his car spun out of control and he plunged into a drift as his engine died. He was truly alone, lost and cold. He began to pray "Please God, help me!" Wondrously, miraculously, he saw coming down the road a brightly lit truck—powerful and sure on the snow-covered road. Behind the wheel was Jesus, alight with a warm radiance that brought inexpressible joy to the man's floundering spirits. "Thank you God!" he cried. The truck pulled up beside the man's car and Jesus got out. To the man's amazement, Jesus got into the man's car beside him. "What is this?" he almost yelled. "I thought you were here to rescue me!" Jesus replied, "I did not come to rescue you from your suffering, but to share it with you."

This story illustrates well the concepts of Connection and control. We all have the capacity to share in each others' suffering, thereby relieving it. Rescue implies an imbalance of power and control. We cannot be responsible adults if we are expecting to be rescued. Sharing is Connection. An imbalance of power and control means that we cannot be truly Connected.

Addictive behavior is about escape and avoidance, but these keep us as emotional and spiritual children. A child believes she is the center of the universe and can control everything. (Of course, *I* was the center of the universe and my sisters will tell you that I still believe that!) All needs and desires must be met and the child is to blame for everything in the world—parents' divorce, abuse, the weather, you name it.

Freud taught us (I don't believe everything that Freud taught, but I believe this theory has proven true) that what happens to a child until the age of five molds his personality forever.

We know that a baby is a helpless creature who relies completely on the caretakers to meet her needs— change a wet diaper, be fed, be held, be warm, be responded to when she cries. A baby whose needs are met fairly consistently and caringly learns, non-verbally, that the world is a safe and caring place. This child has felt a Connection to others from birth. This child will move on through life from this position, with this outlook of basic trust.

On the other hand, a child who is abused or neglected, who cries in his crib and no one comes, who is handled harshly, who is not held and cuddled, will learn that the world is uncaring and unloving. This child will grow up believing that no one will ever meet his needs and no one can be trusted. He will develop a sense of entitlement ("I have a right to meet my needs however I can because no one else will") and disregard of others. Here the basic Disconnect that occurred in infancy is carried on through life. These children may grow up to be criminals and completely without compassion or empathy. Because the message was incorporated on a non-verbal level, it is particularly difficult, if not impossible, to counteract, at least without some intervention (possibly Divine!).

Children who are abused or neglected in subsequent years develop similar traits, known in the psychiatric world as personality disorders. They share, to one degree or another, the sense of the world not being safe and a Disconnect from others. Narcissists try to make their environment in the image they choose—a reflection of what they want others to be—without regard for the individuals with whom they interact. Histrionic personalities create drama so that all attention is on them and they can feel a sense of worth. Borderline personalities see the world as not safe and polarize everything to feel secure. To them, you are either all good or all bad and they can turn on a dime. As long as you are good, they feel safe with you, but do or say something that even slightly shifts their perception, and you are forever bad and not safe to be around. Antisocial personalities are what we used to call sociopaths. They are the individuals who see nothing but their own needs, and the people in their world exist only to meet those needs.

Because relationships are very one-sided for these folks (although their partners and families and friends may not realize the extent of the Disconnect) they tend to engage in addictive behaviors. They do not appreciate how addiction cuts them off from intimacy and Connection and so often have little motivation to change. Recovery is also difficult because they do not have that motivation for Connection that other addicts have to sustain their recovery. As a spiritual person, however, and one who believes that we all have a force within us to evolve spiritually, a force that impels us to Connect, I believe that anyone can attain recovery and Connection.

Certainly not everyone in America has a psychiatric disorder. Most of us have some traits, however, such as a tendency to polarize people or ideas, a sense of entitlement, a tendency toward histrionic behavior, or a desire to control our environment in order to feel safe.

This latter concept applies to just about everyone to some degree or other.

CONTROL VERSUS CONNECTION

Control is a very subtle, oftentimes paradoxical, construct. Most people when they think of control think of telling others what to do, of being the boss, or of being responsible for something or someone. Parents and teachers are seen as being in control, or not being in control, of the children under their care. A job foreman is in control of the workers, and his or her success is measured by their performance and how well the job gets done. Not so obvious are the attempts we all make to control what goes on constantly within ourselves and around us in our environments.

When I rearrange my office furniture, I am controlling my environment in order to feel more at ease and obtain more pleasure from the feng shui in the room. I am also trying to control my clients' state of mind by making the room appear safe and comfortable and to make it a place where they will be able to more readily let down their defenses and open themselves up to me. Coming into my office and sitting in a comfortable, upholstered chair, looking at the photo of the Dalai Lama and the paintings on my walls, and gazing at the fish swimming in their own secluded world, you would probably not describe me as a controlling person, and yet that's what I am attempting to do. Of course, since I do not have any true control over anyone, there is always the possibility that you will not be comfortable on the furniture, you will resent the evidence of my spiritual beliefs, and you may object to holding other living things (the fish, not the client☺) captive for human gratification.

This all goes to show that control is an illusion—unless it is control over ourselves. One of the concepts I try to live by and certainly impart to all of my clients is stated in the Serenity Prayer. It goes: "God, grant me the serenity to accept the things I cannot change, the courage to change the things I can, and the wisdom to know the difference." This goes to the heart of control. We cannot control anything other than ourselves. When we try to, it leads to Disconnection. Therefore, when we are only controlling ourselves, we are open to Connection. Why is this?

Control means that there is a power inequality.

Any time that I say I know better than you, I am putting myself above you. Picture an old-fashioned scale with two weights suspended from a fulcrum. If the weights are balanced, then they are at the same level. Imagine further that the weights are shaped like gears and that when they are balanced they interlock. This is Connection—two interlocking, balanced entities.

Power and control exert weight on our scales, leading to an inability to interlock because one side is higher or lower than the other.

Now imagine (stretch a bit, okay?) that the weights are suspended from a hinge and that they may move farther apart even when level or closer together. This represents our desire for intimacy. We may be level, but we can still swing apart to avoid intimacy.

People find all sorts of ways to avoid intimacy, which of course equates with a desire to control both people and situations. Using substances or activities addictively is a way to control how close we become to others. If I am involved with my addiction, I cannot be involved with you. If I am thinking about how to be stimulated, either through work, the Internet, drugs, shopping or gambling, then I am not thinking about being close to my family or friends.

Addicts are very seldom "present," or in the moment. They are always looking forward to the next thing, thinking about ten minutes or ten weeks from now, but not being aware of what is happening in this moment. As you read this, are you thinking about what will come next or are you really focused on these words now? Are you wondering when the book will end? Are you thinking about what's for dinner or what will happen when you return to work? Take a moment (I'm not going anywhere) to stop and be aware of what is happening right now. Move through each of your senses— sight, hearing, smell, taste, and touch—and just notice what each of them is experiencing. Go ahead, I'll wait.

How often do you allow yourself to do this? Ever? Each moment that we are not in the present is a moment lost in our lives and a moment when we are not Connected. In trying to control a future that does not yet exist, we lose the "now" that does exist. Then when the future arrives, even if we have somehow manipulated it and made it happen as we wanted, we are already on to the next thing, the next high, and so have not really controlled anything because what we really want from any moment is to be happy and feel Connected, and we lose that when we are not in the present.

Connection is only fully realized when we stop and become aware of the moment and allow ourselves to experience another person or our spiritual Connection to all life. So stop, feel, make eye contact, appreciate the air on your skin. Stop and smell the roses and you will feel the Connection. Do you realize that just sharing a commonly known quote like "Stop and smell the roses" forms a Connection between you and me and with everyone who has ever heard or used that phrase? Moreover, the common sense of it makes a Connection with all who understand the meaning even if the expression is new. So you have just Connected with untold millions of people! You are not alone.

CONNECTION AND COMMUNICATION

While we certainly communicate in many non-verbal ways that can be even more powerful than words, language is still the common default for conveying our thoughts and feelings to others. We speak, someone listens, responds, and we listen. In a perfect world, that would be all that is needed to be intimate. However, within that simple concept are a myriad ways to fail to communicate and therefore Disconnect.

As presented with transactional analysis, much of communication is not straightforward but rather ulterior. In other words, we don't say what we mean or we don't ask the question for which we want the answer. For example, Mary might ask her husband, Stan, if he's going to come home on time from work. Already this is not clear communication because what does "on time" mean? Stan might answer, "I don't know, there are some orders coming in, I don't know how late I'll be." Mary could then launch into an attack on Stan about how he's always at work, she never knows what he's up to, why can't he hire someone else to work, and on and on and on. Stan can get defensive and argue his side about how he needs to work to support the family and how could she not know what he's up to and he can't afford to hire anyone else and on and on and on.

Neither of them is saying what they really feel nor are they listening to the other. In fact, they have probably had this argument more times than they can count and it never gets resolved. Why? Because what they are saying is not what is really going on for them. The anger from the argument is keeping distance between them and keeping them Disconnected as they keep trying to control the other in order to feel safe.

Arguments have paradoxical meanings, as so often happens when our Enlightened Brain is having difficulty with the Caveman Brain. They occur when two people both want the other to agree with their point of view, which derives from the fear of not being in control, not being right, or not being important or good enough. Remember, anger is the tip of the fear iceberg. Each one has a fear that underlies their own need to be right because being right will help them feel safe. Arguments also occur as a means to maintain a comfortable distance.

The paradox is that if Stan gave in and said, "Yes, dear, you are absolutely right and I am wrong, I will change," then Mary would need to find another way to continue the argument, because while her Enlightened Brain wants to resolve this issue and feel closer to Stan, her Caveman Brain is saying "Oh no, getting closer is risky and uncomfortable, let's maintain the status quo."

How can Stan and Mary resolve this? First, they need to want to resolve it. Many couples don't think they have a problem, they just like to argue. (Remember, arguing is stimulating and stimulation is addictive.)

If their Enlightened Brains do say, "Hey, let's be more intimate, we can do better here," then they need to agree to work on this common goal, which is to increase intimacy.

Next they can begin to communicate from a more honest, genuine perspective. "I feel" statements are a great way to begin a conversation (or transaction) in a way that will minimize an argument. If Mary can begin the conversation with "I'm feeling lonely and left out of your life when you work late so often. I miss you and would like to spend more time with you," then Stan can respond to her feelings as an "Adult" rather than to an accusation and criticism that taps into his "Child" message of not being good enough. He can then respond with "I feel really anxious when I think about not being able to make our mortgage this month. I really want to spend time with you, but I feel guilty if I spend money to hire someone to do something I can do myself."

Mary and Stan can now take a moment to consider this, to feel the other person and appreciate this intimacy of having shared their fears. From there it is a simple matter to negotiate how to meet both their needs rather than for one to win and the other to lose.

True Listening

Another barrier to communication is when we just don't listen. Our minds are elsewhere, we think we've heard it all before, or we begin to formulate our response before the other person finishes speaking.

There have been many, many times when I have sat with a new couple in my office and each want to tell me their side of the story. I listen to one, we'll call him Stefan, and watch the other, we'll call her Sandra, zone out, completely inattentive. I will mention to Sandra that I guess she has heard this all before and she will roll her eyes and make a face and tell me yes, many times. So then I will ask her to repeat it to me, tell me what Stefan is trying to say, and she will make a feeble start but then be completely lost. Stefan, of course, will say, "See, she doesn't listen!" and he is absolutely right.

People tend to repeat themselves when they do not feel heard or understood. Simply saying "I understand" or "I hear you" does not convey any understanding and will often irritate the speaker. There are a couple of good listening techniques that will indicate that the listener is not only hearing but understanding the speaker—and even more, that the listener genuinely cares about the speaker.

The reflecting technique requires the speaker to first invite the listener to take the time to listen. Stefan can say, "Sandra, I have something important I would like to share with you, when would be a good time?" This will allow Sandra to prepare herself to give Stefan her full attention, as opposed to him throwing out something while she is preparing dinner or answering phone calls. Sandra can then offer a good time to talk, be there as planned, and then give Stefan her full attention as evidenced by making eye contact with him.

Stefan can then speak his thoughts or concerns, beginning with an "I'm feeling" statement. Sandra will be fully present, not letting her mind drift or be thinking of how she wants to respond, but fully focused on what Stefan is sharing, and then she will reflect it back, saying, "What I'm getting from you is…" or "What I'm hearing you say is…" and actually repeating his words back, without ad lib or interpretation and especially without defensiveness. Stefan then can clarify or add to what he wants to convey and Sandra will again reflect his words. When done with the intention of understanding, really "getting" the other person, they will both feel a deeper sense of intimacy and Connection.

The other technique is called **active listening**. It can begin as with the reflection technique, but rather than simply repeating the other person's words, the listener seeks the deeper meaning. Remember the cognitive-behavioral concept of "the way we think leads to how we feel and act?"

Using the earlier example, with active listening Stan will fully take in what Mary is telling him and then respond with what emotion he is getting from her and then with the underlying reason for that emotion, based on what he has heard and also what he knows about her. Stan could say, "You sound hurt because I seem to want to be at work more than I want to be with you." Mary will probably respond with a resounding "Yes!" and then go on to share more of her feelings. Notice that Stan stopped after identifying the underlying reason for Mary's feelings rather than go on to defend himself. Had he defended himself, they would have been right back to arguing over something that isn't the real issue.

When addictive behavior is involved, people find ways to maintain distance through arguing and not sharing feelings. They fear intimacy and also want the excuse to remain in their addiction.

What prevents partners from wanting to listen and be closer to each other?

Couples come together out of an *equal* fear of intimacy. They *both* have that inner child who holds on to the messages of "I'm not good enough," I'm a failure," "I'm a bad person," "I'm worthless," and so on. Each person subliminally recognizes that the other will come so close and no closer, matching each other's comfort level. They will unconsciously strive to keep that distance. For instance, when they are close sexually, they will be emotionally distant. As they become emotionally close, they will pull apart sexually. They will employ any number of mechanisms to maintain the status quo.

Quite commonly, there is one person who is the "identified problem"—often an addict of one sort or another. The partner of the addict has a built-in excuse in the addict for not looking at himself or herself. A few years ago, I worked with a couple, Sergio and Alexa (definitely not their real names). Sergio was new in recovery and had completed a residential rehabilitation program. He and Alexa came to me complaining of a lack of intimacy in their relationship. They both agreed they wanted to be closer, more Connected, but when I asked if they would like to do a basic intimacy-building communication exercise (the reflecting technique), Alexa almost knocked her chair over in her anxiousness to pull away. Although she had presented complaining about the lack of intimacy over the years and firmly stated that she wanted to be closer to Sergio, she was adamant in her refusal to take even the smallest step in that direction.

Sergio, because of the negative consequences of his behavior, had been forced to face the fact that his life was out of control. He had no place to hide, and so he began the work of recovery. He saw how spiritually rewarding life in recovery could be and ventured into the incredibly difficult work of confronting his demons and healing the old wounds. He was now ready to build a more loving, present, and Connected relationship with his wife.

Alexa, on the other hand, was so afraid of looking within herself and dealing with whatever losses or rejections she had experienced in childhood that she clung frantically to her anger towards Sergio. Her anger provided a level of stimulation to her brain that was addictive as well. As in any addiction, the stimulation provided a relief from her old pain. Sergio's past addictive behavior gave her the excuse to not face her own issues, and so she had to maintain the distance between them with blame. Until she took responsibility for herself and the subliminal reasons she was initially attracted to Sergio, they could not move forward as a couple. If Sergio continued to allow her to do this, she would eventually sabotage his recovery and he would relapse.

Some partners *are* able to recognize that they have their own work to do to become capable of intimacy, but some hold tight to their defenses and remain fixed in their anger, which provides the stimulation to feed their own addictive minds.

*Couples come together out of
an equal fear of intimacy!*

PSEUDO-INTIMACY

This drive for intimacy that our spiritual selves crave coupled with the fear of intimacy from the Caveman Brain often impels us to engage in pseudo-intimate relationships.

Remember the television series "Cheers?" A friendly bar full of regular characters who were all seemingly good pals. For many years, I was a bartender (short jump to becoming a counselor, some might say). I enjoyed the fun of being where most people go to socialize and relax while earning money at the same time. After the excitement of beginning in a new place wore off, though, and I got to know the patrons, I would notice a phenomenon that was common to every bar in which I ever worked, which is that there are regulars who hang out almost every night and refer to the bar as their "home away from home" or even call it their "real home." I and the other bartenders and wait staff and (depending on the bar, I admit I have worked in some varied establishments) dancers were lovingly referred to as "family." But let's face it, we were not these folks' family members, we were employees and the patrons were paying us. Yes, I liked some of them, sort of, but if I didn't have to earn a living, I would have been home with my own family or spending time with my real friends. Of course, these bar regulars were all alcoholics and I found myself in the uncomfortable position of being nice and pouring drinks for tips while being fully aware of enabling someone's addiction. Take away the humor and drama written into the TV show and even Cheers was a pretty sad place. Cliff was a lonely mailman living with his mother and Norm had a wife at home that he apparently avoided like the plague. Sam and Carla, the bartenders, often made it evident that they would not have relationships with these men if it was not part of their job. It was why I changed jobs so often and eventually became a counselor, putting me on the other side of the bar, so to speak, and healing rather than enabling.

People engage in any number of pseudo-intimate relationships, as when they go to a casino and gamble and get on a first-name basis with the dealers, or they feel some connection (*not* a capital "c") with the regular hosts on the home shopping channels, or go to sports events and yell endearments (or epithets) to the players.

Pseudo-intimacy is something we can control, while true intimacy can feel out of control. In a pseudo-intimate relationship, I control how close I get, how much information I divulge, how much of a façade I show you versus my true self.

Sex is very often a pseudo-intimate act. Eyes meet across a room, sparks fly, two people are drawn to each other like characters from a Victorian romance. Their prefrontal cortices (not particularly enlightened at this moment) explain the flood of dopamine by saying they must have known each other in a past life, they must be soul mates, and they have the right chemistry for an enduring love affair and so on. They engage in mad, passionate sex and begin to share those select pieces of personal information that are most likely to present them in a favorable light. They find something about the other person on which they can build a fantasy. (I once fell for a guy in a band because of his cowboy hat. He turned out to be an alcoholic. When he staggered out to his car, totally intoxicated and tried to drive away, my brief infatuation was over.)

Couples who continue with the fantasy and form a relationship will often find that, when the sexual passion wanes (usually in about six months, give or take) they have nothing on which to continue to build intimacy. They have confused sexual relations with intimacy and true Connection and will sometimes seek therapy to get back their sex lives. It is then that I discuss the true meaning of intimacy, which is to feel fully Connected and open and to feel bonded emotionally, intellectually, socially, recreationally, and spiritually. I have yet to find a couple who did not intuitively "get" this concept and agree to at least

When sex is used as a short-cut to intimacy, it only leads to a dead end. When intimacy is developed over time and is the result of true Connection, sex will be an expression of that intimacy and will always be wonderful and new!

try to change their approach to their lives and take their relationship to a new level. When they begin this journey, how often they are having sex becomes far less important than the quality of the interaction.

Remember, couples come together out of an equal fear of intimacy. Our Enlightened Brains want to be intimate, but our Caveman Brains push against it, and so we search out pseudo-intimate relationships in an ultimately fruitless attempt to find true Connection. What's to be done?

The Universe is always working for us and with us! Partners are the catalysts for each others' healing, growth, and spiritual evolution. We seek out, find, and love those people who cause us the most distress, but through our love we have this amazing opportunity to work on those barriers to intimacy that have prevented Connection. We can choose to heal the old traumas and live lives of incredible peace, spiritual prosperity, and enlightenment.

PART III:
RECOVERY AND
CONNECTION

CHARITY VERSUS SELFISHNESS –
IS THERE A DIFFERENCE?

Though I speak with the tongues of men and of angels, and have not charity, I am become as sounding brass, or a tinkling cymbal.

And though I have the gift of prophecy, and understand all mysteries, and all knowledge; and though I have all faith, so that I could remove mountains, and have not charity, I am nothing.

And though I bestow all my goods to feed the poor, and though I give my body to be burned, and have not charity, it will profit me nothing.

Charity suffers long, and is kind; charity envies not; charity vaunts not itself, is not puffed up,

Does not behave itself unseemly, seeks not her own, is not easily provoked, thinks no evil;

Rejoices not in iniquity, but rejoices in the truth;

Bears all things, believes all things, hopes all things, endures all things.

Charity never fails: but whether there be prophecies, they shall fail; whether there be tongues, they shall cease; whether there be knowledge, it shall vanish away.

For we know in part, and we prophesy in part.

But when that which is perfect is come, then that which is in part shall be done away.

When I was a child, I spoke as a child, I understood as a child, I thought as a child: but when I became a man, I put away childish things.

For now we see through a glass, darkly; but then face to face: now I know in part; but then shall I know even as also I am known.

And now abides faith, hope, charity, these three; but the greatest of these is charity.

The Book of 1st Corinthians: Chapter 13

The word "charity" has gotten a bad rap over the years. When we think of charity, we think of alms for the poor, giving donations to charitable organizations, or just generally giving away something that we don't need or have extra of and don't want to feel guilty and we want the tax benefit.

There is something demeaning in giving this way. When we donate our clothes and goods that we no longer want or need, we are secretly grateful that we are on the giving and not on the receiving end. We have a complacence and smugness that says "I would never be in a position where I would need to use someone else's blender or dress in someone else's clothes." We give more from a feeling of guilt that, as Americans, we are a wasteful society and at least if we give away our stuff rather than throw it away, we're not quite so wasteful. We can better justify buying some new toy.

Americans can be wasteful, make no mistake, and the wastefulness of American culture is woven into the fabric of addiction. It has become a natural part of the fabric of our society that we buy more than we need, get tired of it, and move on to the next technological innovation. Appliances and technological toys are made to break in a way that makes them more expensive to fix than to replace. We even have a name for this: planned obsolescence. Businesses and companies are the drug dealers of our techno world. They get us hooked on the pleasure of a new gadget and then intensify the effects so we crave more and more, which they are happy to supply.

Our technology upgrades so quickly that it is a full-time job just learning how to use it all. I had finally begun to buy CDs and build a collection when everything went to iPods and MP3s. I had just bought a turntable to turn my old albums into CDs when, before I had a chance to learn the software for the conversion, the system was obsolete. Now I find that, if I give in to it, I can purchase some new techno toy for half the price of the last one to convert the music from my albums onto an iPod. Will I give in to the new or doggedly stick with the old? With all the musical options now available in the form of satellite radio, I seldom listen to my CDs anyway. It's all too much!

All this buying and upgrading with its consequent immediate self-gratification is yet another form of addiction. Think about the criteria for dependence from the DSM—tolerance and withdrawal, efforts to cut down, a great deal of time spent, important activities given up, and continuation in spite of exacerbating an existing problem. We started out with personal computers and then began the upgrades as new software and games overwhelmed the hardware capabilities of our systems. Then laptops and MP3s and iPods, then smart phones. We need more to get the same effect and we feel anxious when we don't have the latest technology. We spend time researching the technology, shopping for it, trying out everything. We say that we will stop after this next toy but we don't. We spend money that we don't have or that could be spent better on something more substantial.

All this taking in, filling the hole, seeking that next high. This is addiction.

Children now spend their leisure time in malls rather than parks or playgrounds. They are surrounded by an excess of material goods that was unheard of thirty years ago. Personally, I get claustrophobic and overwhelmed with the sheer magnitude of the clothes, electronics, and toys in malls today. Of course, to avoid that, I end up shopping online, which is a far more solitary and sedentary activity and for many, far more addictive.

As you can recognize, this kind of excess and instant gratification are the basis for addiction. We need more and more to get the same effect (tolerance) and feel anxious, irritable, and depressed when we are deprived of the activity (withdrawal). We are creating whole generations of addicts with the mindless glut of products and activities available today. Our young people are learning that nothing is ever enough to satisfy them, no amount of possessions or money will ever be enough, but they will still chase the next dollar and the next toy so there can be just a moment of satisfaction.

I worked for a time with juveniles who had ended up in a halfway house due to criminal activity of some sort, whether from shoplifting, stealing cars, selling drugs, or burglarizing houses. I asked one young man, a pretty intelligent, well-spoken individual of seventeen, why he did it. His reply appalled me. He said that he needed money for new sneakers. His mother provided perfectly adequate footwear for him, but it was not the $200 designer sneakers in vogue at the time and to which he felt entitled. It is that sense of entitlement that is at the heart of much of our addiction. The idea is that because something is the norm in whatever circle in which we move, we are then entitled to it.

This young man was at the mercy of his group, remember. Children who do not wear the "right" clothing or otherwise follow the rules will be exiled. Peer pressure is powerful and taps into the deepest motivators of our behavior—the need to belong. There is a very basic dissatisfaction with ourselves and our circumstances when we cannot "keep up with the Joneses" as we used to say. The concept of internal versus external locus of control and validation is at work here. It is easier to feel good about oneself if one has the $200 sneakers or the Mercedes or the designer clothes than if one has to look within at one's personal abilities and attributes.

Taken to an extreme, mob behavior is an example of the need to belong to the group even to the extent that the most fundamental personal values will be violated. Our history in the United States is full of stories of massacres, lynchings, witch burnings, and other violent behavior that, were the individual to have been acting independently, these acts would never occur. It is the need to belong, exacerbated by the stimulation of the mob excitement (back to dopamine and friends) that Disconnects the limbic system from the Enlightened Brain and the individual from the higher power.

The American Dream—what is it? Something different for each of us to some extent, but shared by each generation. For many immigrants, it is an opportunity to work for oneself and profit from one's labors. It is an opportunity to ensure that one's children will live a better life. For the next generation, it becomes a way of life to which one is entitled just by virtue of being an American. In my work, I meet parents all the time who bemoan the fact that their children lack their own work ethic yet, when asked how the children would have learned that work ethic, they are at a loss. They are surprised when I point out that the parenting they received was what taught them their ethics, but they had not provided that learning or those experiences to their own children. Why, then, would they expect their children to appreciate money and possessions and have a sense of community when their children never had to work for those things?

Parents from the Great Depression (as mine were) and many parents who have emigrated from other countries have lived with poverty. They learned to value what they had and to turn to other members of the community for support through their hard times. These parents vowed that their children would never suffer the hardships that they had, and so gave them money, clothes, and an education with no strings. How, then, would these children learn to value what was given to them?

The result of all this freedom is generations with a sense of entitlement, who feel resentful and empty if they don't get what they *think* is owed to them. The focus on material possessions and money leaves them with spiritual deprivation as well. It was well said in the Bible that it is easier for a camel to go through the eye of a needle than for a rich man to get into heaven. The more focused we are on the material world, the less attention we give to our own spirits.

All of which brings us back to the concept of charity. Charity is a giving of oneself, of one's energy and goodness, an acknowledgement of the Connection we all share. When I give to you in a truly charitable sense, I am not thinking of myself, and so paradoxically I become enriched in the process. Being charitable is actually a selfish act! If I am fully Connected to others, then I feel their pain. Wanting to stop that pain is really for my benefit as much as theirs. It is heartening today to find that many schools are incorporating community service into their curriculum, thereby instilling a sense of Connection and realization of the fulfillment that comes from serving others.

Addicts are always focused on themselves—when can I get my next fix, how can I be stimulated? Charity is a means to get out of oneself, to give one's brain a rest. Think about a time when you were fully engaged in an activity helping someone. You were not thinking about yourself—about your aches and pains, your money problems, what you had to do at work the next day. Your charitable activity was of benefit to you, maybe more so than it was to the person you were helping.

Some time ago, I was working with a sex addict who happened to be a major sports star. He had the beautiful wife and children, the fabulous career, tons of money and all of the paraphernalia that goes with it, yet he was perpetually focused on himself. He was, however, on a spiritual progression that was helping him to want more real Connection in his life. He came to therapy not just because his wife caught him cheating (although that was the initial motivator) but because he was realizing that life was more than just the outward manifestations of success.

One day he told me a very moving story. He had been at a gas station, pumping gas into his very classy car, when a homeless man approached him for a handout. My client of course gave him some money, but more significant, he looked at him full in the face, eyeball to eyeball, and talked to him, something he never would have done before recovery. He didn't say much, just "hello, how are you doing," something along those lines, but the effect was electric. As he told me later, the homeless man lit up, smiled, and thanked him for talking to him, for acknowledging his existence. So often we ignore the beggars on the street corners or, if we do give them something, we never make eye contact or say a word. In his quest for Connection as part of his recovery, my client gave a gift that had far reaching effects for not only the homeless individual, but for himself, for me, for my other clients and students, and now for everyone who reads these words.

For those of us who are not celebrities, let's not underestimate the worth of our impact on others. Every encounter with another person is an opportunity to get outside of ourselves and give something of value—a smile, a word, a compliment, a touch.

These days, we casually talk about our lack of personal interactions. I hear many people say that they don't know their neighbors, and I watch them walk down the street without making eye contact. I watch the expressions ranging from preoccupation to suspicion to aloofness. When I go walking now, I smile and say hello or good morning to everyone I pass and then observe the start they give and the answering smile. Connection, recovery, and an elevation to a higher plane, this is the gift we give ourselves and others when we get outside of our own heads and exercise charity.

THE CONNECTION OF SUFFERING

L ast year I had reached a point in my life where I thought I pretty much had everything together— my marriage, my career, my finance—and I thought that, barring some crisis, my suffering in this lifetime was pretty much behind me. I thought that the struggles through which I had gone were over and I could sit placidly and listen to my clients' painful stories, hear my friends with a certain (I admit it) smugness, and that my life in future would be one of creativity and personal enjoyment. Then about a year ago I became depressed, almost overnight it seemed. I lost all inter- est and enjoyment in life, lost all satisfaction in my work. My personal relationships became shadowy and unfocused and all I wanted to do was escape from my life—not through suicide, but just to step out, run away, go live in a forest somewhere and eat nuts and berries. I realized that I had felt this way a few times in my life and it was always at a time when I was going through some change of life. Just when my life seemed to be altogether, I needed it to change. I needed to be challenged, to find some new meaning and purpose, some new way to use all the skills and education and experience I had gained—or so I thought.

I questioned myself, looking for some reason for why I had to go through this. I struggled with wanting *to do* something that would make me feel better. I tried to think of something that would engage me, something that I could throw myself into and that would provide the stimulation that would get me out of my funk.

Whoa! Does this sound familiar? One day when I was twisting and turning like a bug on a pin, I just stopped. I realized that I didn't have *to do* anything—I could just take one day at a time, be in the moment, and enjoy each moment. Everything that I told my clients every day I needed to do myself. Walk the walk, not just talk the talk, as they say in Alcoholics Anonymous. It's ok to not be doing all the time and it's ok to *just be*.

Then I found a quiet place to just sit quietly and be with myself and to Connect with the Universe, as I have done at times in the past, and the answer to my unasked question of why I had to experience this depression came as always, simple and clear. It is through suffering that we connect with each other. As I sat in a session with a client who was feeling very depressed, I had a new appreciation for her pain and realized that I had become a bit complacent and that through my own depression I could more fully experience her world and be not so quick with strategies to remedy her situation. Pain and suffering in life are inevitable. Addiction is an escape from that pain and suffering, but it is the sharing that brings us to each other and closer to that synergy for which there are so many names. We must live it, go through it, *and not* escape from it, in order to evolve as human beings.

While writing this book, I met a woman who happened to have been a midwife for many years. She shared with me her own story of having lost her baby and how this experience, as painful as it was, gave her a deeper Connection with the women with whom she worked. She was and is an incredibly spiritual person who is very much attuned to nature and the Universe, and her relating of this story in response to reading a draft of this book is an affirmation that this kind of Connection is real, it exists, and it can be felt by all who open themselves to others.

We are often uncomfortable with others' suffering. When our friends or family members are feeling blue, we want to cheer them up. We tell them to not feel bad, that things will get better, that everything is for a reason. Such advice is not only useless; it usually causes the recipient to feel either more depressed or to get angry. We don't feel Connected or understood when someone is telling us to feel better. They are denying our pain and that causes distance. The advice is a form of drug: Take this pill and feel better. The message is clear: it is not acceptable to feel pain and one must remove or pacify the pain as quickly as possible so everyone is happy.

The parable of Jesus and the snowplow demonstrates how sharing pain is the greatest gift we can offer. It is through our own suffering and experience of passing through it that we are able to endure another person's pain. When we pacify our own suffering, we don't learn that we can survive and therefore we are not able to tolerate others' suffering. We try to "make" them feel better and only give the message that pain and suffering are something to escape, and so the addictive cycle continues.

HEALING AND RECOVERY

Healing and recovery are about Connection.

In 1935 in Akron Ohio, Bill Wilson and Dr. Bob Smith (Bill W. and Dr. Bob) created the fellowship that we know as Alcoholics Anonymous as a way for addicts to help addicts. The premise is simple: those that have been there know best how to help others suffering from the same affliction. The Twelve Steps were written as a guide to not only give up addiction and remain in recovery, but to live a better life overall— more Connected and spiritual.

I have heard recovering addicts say that their worst day sober is better than their best day high. This belief that being sober is better than being under the influence of drugs is what keeps addicts in recovery. Many addicts stop using because of an immediate consequence or fear of a consequence, such as losing a spouse or going to jail, but that never keeps them in recovery. I have seen many addicts relapse by doing something for which they know there will be some horrible consequence, like prison or divorce, yet relapse they do.

They will say that "it just happened" or "I couldn't think of anything else," but when we look at what preceded the relapse, we can easily see that there was some depression or despair, some lack of belief that life would indeed be better. For many, they have never known life without addiction and so have no frame of reference, no belief in something they have never experienced. For those people who were abused or neglected as children, for whom the basic needs of life were never provided, it is difficult to believe that there is something better than that next high out there.

My path crossed with a very special man while I was working in the jail. He was in his late thirties and had been using cocaine all of his adult life and alcohol and marijuana since age eleven. His parents had given him and his brother up for adoption because they could not afford to raise him—sounds like some Grimm fairy tale—and he was sent to live with a couple who were well-intentioned but physically and emotionally abusive. He began getting into trouble immediately and his life, already not great, went downhill. When I met him, he had already killed a man while under the influence of intravenous cocaine and had become addicted to crack while on a work release program. He had spent years on the streets, living by stealing and prostituting himself. He ate garbage and slept under bushes. What better life could he envision? How could this man have a belief that life could be better without drugs when he had never experienced it?

The answer lies, of course, in Connection, in the universal knowing what life can be. Life being good is not about the external factors, it is about the inner feelings of peace and love that we all have the capacity to experience as human beings. When this man Connected with me he felt, for the first time, the joy of unconditional acceptance, and it awakened in him a desire for more. It was only when frustration and hopelessness overcame him that he lost sight of this and relapsed on cocaine. He needed to feel the Connection to all life, not just to me.

As Victor Frankl discovered, it is up to each of us to find meaning in life. I must trust that this man's life is in God's hands and he will find his way back to sobriety and Connection. This was a life lesson for me as well, as I had to learn that I could not control this man or "make" him live the life I thought was right for him. I had to "Let go and let God" as they say in A.A.

Many years ago, I was working in a restaurant that employed immigrants from behind the Iron Curtain— the countries that were under Communist dictatorships from the end of World War II through the late "80s. I met a twenty-year-old man from Romania who told me how he came to the United States. When he was sixteen, he ran away in the middle of the night and began swimming the river that separated Romania from Yugoslavia. The police saw him and began shooting at him, and he was picked up and thrown in prison for six months, given only bread and water. When he was released, he immediately began planning his escape again, even knowing that he would be killed if caught.

This time he was able to swim the two miles across the river, and then he travelled across Yugoslavia by night, sleeping in hay stacks during the day and eating what he could scavenge. Finally he crossed into Italy, where he was received by a refugee station. He came to the U.S. speaking no English and without friends, family, or resources. I asked him why, when he had never known any other life, he would risk his life in this way. He replied that he and his friends "just knew" that freedom existed and they all had a longing for it. One does not have to experience something to know that it exists, and so it is with our longing for Connection.

WE ARE ALL IN RECOVERY

I began this book with the definition of addiction: Obsessive, compulsive, out of control behavior done in spite of negative consequences to self and others. We have explored the meaning of this definition. Obsession is a preoccupation with something that is yet to come, that is in the future, and over which we have no control. Compulsive behavior is motivated by the needs of the limbic system to maintain the elevated baseline that developed from an artificially enhanced stimulant. Out of control means that the behavior is done even when one is trying to make a conscious choice not to do it. Negative consequences are anything that are barriers to intimacy and Connection in any way, shape, or form.

The definition of recovery, then, is being present, being at peace with simple and natural pleasures, being able to control one's inner world with no need to control the external world, and feeling Connected to each other, all life, and the Universe.

I believe that we are all part of a spiritual evolution that takes place within each of us as we grow more aware of our Connection. Just as a caveman cannot build a computer because he lacks all the gathered knowledge of subsequent generations, neither can we attain spiritual growth without the wisdom of all the souls who have come before and who are in the world with us now. Individually we are limited by our own senses and experiences; collectively, through Connection, we have all knowledge already within us. Furthermore, our growth and evolution is limited by those who are still struggling with the spiritual tasks some of us may have mastered, just as we are holding back those who have moved beyond us. The Dalai Lama is an example of someone who chooses to walk among us as a teacher and living example of enlightenment. He will not move forward on his spiritual evolution until all of us are able to move forward as well.

"Love your enemy," "Do unto others as you would have them do unto you," "Send not for whom the bell tolls, it tolls for thee"—these are our messages from the Universe that guide us to Connection. The concepts of intimacy, charity, the Tree of Life, and the Force—these provide the framework within which we may embrace our ties to each other and spiritually evolve.

I wrote this book as my way of bringing people together. What I have learned in my own spiritual evolution I have shared with friends and clients and now share with you.

We are Connected.

GIFTS

I consider myself a fortunate person. I have been fortunate in that I have always had a roof over my head, food to eat, have never lacked money for what I needed, and, most important, I have been loved. I live in a country where I have had opportunities to grow and develop both intellectually and spiritually.

The gifts from the Universe with which I have been blessed are what allow me to help others. I have been given love and I give love, I have been forgiven and so I can forgive, and I have felt pain from innumerable losses and so can feel others' pain and know that we can all survive. Some time ago I began a daily ritual of giving thanks to the Universe for what I receive and for what I am able to give, and this grounds me and puts my life into perspective.

When I get caught up in my own addictive behavior, running about in an increasing state of being stressed and overwhelmed, this grounding ritual allows me to step out of the craziness, Connect with the Universe, and remember what is important in life.

I also realize that I could, indeed, lose everything at any time. A hurricane could wipe out my home. A devastating illness could strike me or someone I love. What I am learning is to be present. Today I have these gifts that I can share. Today I have what I need, and I have the faith from Connection that, whatever happens, I will have what I need tomorrow. I create meaning in life each day.

This book is my gift to you. It is not enough for me to gather the knowledge and insights contained here and keep them to myself or even just share them with those who walk through my door. I feel like a conduit, or maybe a neurotransmitter, passing on to you those gifts of knowledge and awareness that have come to me. Please accept them, use them, build on them, and then pass them on in your turn. This is how we all Connect.

PART IV: CONNECTION WORKBOOK

YOUR DAILY CONNECTION GUIDE

Connection is what our spirits instinctually crave, but it does not come naturally to our modern American souls. We must begin with the intention to Connect and then practice on a daily basis. The following exercises will help you to practice and experience Connection in your life. It may be difficult at first as you detox and withdraw from the stress and stimulation of your addictive existence, but you will discover each day the peace and joy that comes from the security of belonging to all life, of being Connected to all who have ever lived and will continue to live in our universe.

We are holistic beings and therefore need to attend to our physical, intellectual, and spiritual selves. Our emotional selves encompass all of these, as the feelings of joy and peace will accompany us whenever we are Connected and present.

As you practice each exercise, allow yourself to first be aware of the mental and physical quality of your being and then be aware of the spiritual experience. Notice your body—your sense of smell, sight, sound, and sensation. Pay attention to how your mind is processing the experience and take joy in knowing that you are growing and evolving. Finally, feel yourself expanding outside the bounds of your body and senses. Let your spirit connect the earth and sky and feel it mingle with all other life as the breath you exhale mingles with the air that envelops the entire earth and is breathed by all other living beings.

As you breathe, bring the air through your nose, into your lungs, and then down into your diaphragm. Imagine it moving in a circular motion so that inhaling and exhaling is a continuous motion. Feel the breath filling all parts of your body so you become light and energized. Feel your Connection with the Universe.

CONNECTING WITH YOUR INNER SELF

APPRECIATION

For this exercise, you may want to find a talisman on which to focus your appreciation of the blessings the Universe has given you. You can choose a figure such as a Buddha, Ganesh, or Kuan Yin. You may prefer a tree or flower, a stream, lake, or ocean.

Turn slowly in a circle and be aware of the energy flow as you face different directions. When it feels right, face in that direction with your talisman in front of you. You may sit or stand. Bow to the talisman with your hands together, fingers upward. Begin breathing deeply into your diaphragm and be aware of the air as it comes into your body and fills you completely, then as you exhale, feel the air leaving you to mingle with all the air around the planet.

As you inhale, give thanks for what has been given to you. Feel yourself taking in the blessings and gifts. You may keep it general or give thanks for something in particular. It could be something concrete, like money you received or a new car, but it will be more meaningful if you give thanks for whatever enabled you to be the recipient of the gift. For instance, the intellect that allowed you to get the job that enabled you to make the money or buy the car. It becomes more meaningful when you can give thanks for the love you have in your life or the help someone has given to you.

As you inhale, bring your hands, still connected and cupped as if you were going to scoop up water, and bring the gifts into you. Then move them in a circular motion as you exhale and imagine your breath also coming into you and leaving you in an unending circle rather than just in and out. Repeat this at least three times.

Now allow your hands to extend as if in offering as you exhale. Your focus is on giving thanks for the gifts that you have to give others. Bring the air up from your diaphragm and follow with your hands as you extend them and allow your breath to go out with your thanks to mingle with the air. You may choose to focus on a particular gift or recipient and imagine yourself breathing toward that person or persons. You may just give thanks to the Universe that you are able to be giving thanks! That you have the awareness to be on this path of spiritual evolution and that you are aware of your Connection. Do this at least three times, and then bow again to your talisman.

Allow yourself time in the moment to experience how you are feeling.

INTENTION FOR A GOOD DAY

The power of intention is strong indeed. Begin each day with this pledge:

This Day
  Will be a good day
  I will be present and mindful
  I will smile at everyone
  I will listen to others and understand their world
  I will nurture myself with good food, exercise, and fresh air
  I will be nurtured with hugs and smiles
  I will trust in the good intentions of those who love me
  I will send Light to anyone from whom I perceive harm
  I will be the person I want to be
  I will be Connected

CONNECTING WITH OTHERS

SPREAD THE LIGHT

Choose at least one person (more is better) each day with whom to Connect. It could be your partner, your child, a co-worker, or anyone on the street. Take a moment to smile and make eye contact, then say "Hello, how are you today?" Ask with the *intention of really wanting to know* how this person is feeling and what he or she is experiencing. If the person responds with a simple "I'm fine, and you?" then reply with a feeling statement, such as "I feel wonderful" or "I feel quite well, thank you." If the person responds with "I'm not feeling well" or "I had some bad news," then you can say "I'm sorry to hear that, I will (insert what you are comfortable saying: pray, think about you, send you good energy, hope things get better, etc.)." Remember, you do not need to solve anyone's problems, only share the emotion and Connect.

REFLECTING AND ACTIVE LISTENING

Use a reflecting or active listening response to someone every day.

"What I hear you saying is _____."

"You sound _ (feeling word)_ because _(underlying belief about the situation)._"

Remember, you DO NOT need to solve the problem or give advice. You are just letting the person know you care and understand by giving the gift of listening.

CREATE HEALTHY BOUNDARIES
BOUNDARIES WITH EACH OTHER

We need boundaries in our relationships. This is often confusing in addiction and recovery because people think of boundaries as something Disconnecting. In reality, healthy boundaries allow us to be aware of ourselves and others as individuals who are autonomous. We are all responsible for ourselves—our thoughts, feelings, and behavior. The concepts of individuality and responsibility relate back to those of control and equality. We can only be truly Connected and intimate when we are not trying to control each other. When you feel as if you are trying to control another person's feelings or behavior, or when you are feeling taken advantage of or controlled, you need to look at your boundaries. Take care of yourself, be assertive, and recite the Serenity Prayer:

God, grant me the serenity to accept the things I cannot change,
the courage to change the things I can, and
the wisdom to know the difference.

BOUNDARIES IN DAILY LIVING

Addiction is a barrier to intimacy, so we need to create boundaries that will allow us space in which to be intimate and Connected. Do an inventory of your day and find those behaviors that are addictive and put boundaries around them. For instance:

- Make an agreement with your partner that there will be no laptops or cell phones at the dinner table or in the bedroom.
- Create and adhere to scheduled times for activities.
- Allow yourself uninterrupted time to work on daily tasks; for example, do not answer the phone while working on a report.

When you have established healthy boundaries with others, then you will be present and Connected within that space you create in which to be with them.

RECOVERY EXERCISES

FLOAT OUT OF THE RIP TIDE

A rip tide is an ocean current that is not visible from the surface because of breezes that ruffle the surface water and hide the outgoing tide below. When people get caught in a rip tide that sweeps them out to sea, their inclination is to swim against it as they try to get to shore. The rip tide is too powerful to swim against, though, so people often panic and exhaust themselves and ultimately drown.

The secret is to not swim against the tide, but to let your body float above it. There on the surface you can gently paddle parallel to the shore until you are out of the rip tide. Then you can swim with the waves and make it to shore.

Addiction is like a rip tide—you cannot directly fight it. The very act of fighting provides the stimulation that feeds the addiction. When you find yourself craving food or drugs or sex or gambling, when you find yourself getting into pointless arguments or compulsively working or your cell phone is glued to your hand, ***don't fight it!*** Imagine yourself floating up and above the rip tide, just relaxing and being in the moment. Feel yourself gently float away as you just breathe. When you feel the rip tide no longer tugging at you, then look around and see where you are and make a decision where you want to be. Then gently swim in that direction.

GET A HOBBY

A hobby has a paradoxical purpose. While you are working on it, the purpose is to be fully engaged, fully present, so that your brain waves can settle down. It is important not to be thinking about getting it done, but to be experiencing the process—enjoy the ride.

Conversely, when you *are* finished, you have something to hold and appreciate, to say "I did this!" It can be wonderfully satisfying.

Find a hobby that involves using your hands, such as building a birdhouse out of popsicle sticks. It does not have to be difficult. In fact, simpler is better, since some people's addictive natures can overwhelm the intention of the hobby, as when someone I knew became obsessed with building a model ship and the detail and intricacy overwhelmed him and he quit. So keep it simple, at least to start. A jigsaw puzzle, paint by numbers, basic model airplane, mosaic tile trivet (that was my father's in rehab—I still have it) cross-stitch, or anything else that holds an interest for you.

If you are in a relationship, then doing a hobby together can build intimacy with your partner.

FELLOWSHIP

Twelve-step anonymous meetings are helpful for many people. They are a place where you know you will be fully accepted, where you can safely (and anonymously) share your most shameful secrets and begin to heal, and where you will learn from other addicts about how to live a recovering lifestyle. You will find a sponsor who will be your guide and help you work through the twelve steps, which are applicable for everyone who wants to live an open, Connected life.

So what about those of you who are saying, "But I don't have an addiction to drugs or sex or gambling. There's no twelve-step meeting for cell phone addicts or workaholics or gaming addicts."

You can still use the underlying intention of twelve-step meetings in your life. Find a group of friends with whom you can socialize on a regular basis and do so with the intention of creating a fellowship of like-minded people—those who are also seeking Connection and intimacy and simple enjoyment of life.

You can use any number of existing groups as well: by joining a book club or taking martial arts lessons or classes that will help you with your hobby. Then Connect with some people who seem amenable and build from there.

THOUGHT STOPPING

Every so often we all experience those times when our minds race and we can't stop or when we obsess about something. Obsession, of course, is part of addiction, and our obsessing provides the stimulation that our addict brains are craving, often leading to acting out. How can we stop?

Certainly not by getting into an argument with ourselves. That only leads to more stimulation, and since we are ultimately powerless over our addiction, we will eventually lose the fight.

Instead, a simple way of dealing with this is to recite a memorized, meaningful poem or prayer and be fully focused on it. Personally, the Lord's Prayer works for me. I pay attention to each line and attend to the inherent meaning in the words. Repeating this two or three times moves me out of the obsessive thinking and grounds me to the present.

Find something that works for you that is inspiring, spiritual, and enlightening.

STRUCTURE YOUR DAY

I was talking with a food addict the other day, and she told me that she obsesses all day about what she will eat for dinner that night. I told her to just plan her meal ahead of time and forget about it. She loved it!

We act addictively when we have time on our hands and a lack of structure. If planning your day sounds boring, that is your addict mind talking. It can be very freeing to know what you are doing. Remember the locus of control. You can decide what you want to do and, more importantly, how you want *to be* today and you can let the rest go.

As part of your daily routine, examine your food, exercise, and relaxation habits.

Eliminate artificial sweeteners, sugar, and caffeine.

Artificial sweeteners are addictive and will cause you to crave more food, especially foods high in sugar and carbohydrates. "All things in moderation" is the key. Don't deprive yourself of foods you like, just balance them with other, healthy foods and take smaller portions of everything. Drink water and unsweetened tea. Use honey as a sweetener. It has antibiotic properties, and eating local honey is said to reduce allergies.

Go out in the sun for at least twenty minutes per day.

Many Americans suffer from Vitamin D deprivation due to lack of sun or lathering on sunscreen when they go out. In addition to providing Vitamin D, sun is a mood elevator and also stimulates the production of melatonin, the natural chemical that promotes sleep. It helps to give yourself a break during the day by getting out of the office and soaking up some rays. Literally Be In Light!

Exercise each day.

Find a variety of activities that you enjoy and do one or two daily. Mix up aerobic with weight-bearing exercises. Go for a walk, a swim, or a bike ride. Go to the gym or take a martial arts or yoga class. Vary your routine but schedule something every day.

Drink chamomile tea to relax.

There are many teas that can help with whatever ails you. Chamomile is especially helpful with relaxing, whether it is during the day when you need a break or in the evening when you are unwinding before bed.

Do not take any sleep aids.

Even over-the-counter sleep aids can become addictive. When you take something to sleep, you set up the cycle of thinking you need it to sleep, and then your Caveman Brain just keeps you awake until you take that magic pill. Melatonin is already in your brain, so while you are detoxing from the other drugs, it can help you relax naturally so you can get back to sleeping on your own. Remember to get out in the sun so your brain can produce its own melatonin. You may also need to spend a few sleepless nights while you detox and get your brain accustomed to the idea that it will not get its fix. The "Rip Tide" exercise can help with this as well. Don't struggle with sleep, just notice what is happening and float above it.

Schedule relaxation time.

We become so driven with the idea that we need to be doing something productive every waking moment that we feel guilty if we stop. Schedule yourself some time each day to just relax. This can be your time in the sun or your time to sit in the garden and drink your chamomile tea or time to just stare into space. It allows your brainwaves to calm down. It allows you to Connect to the Universe. It allows you to just be. Remember to turn off your cell phone!

Affirmation Rituals

Affirmation rituals help to ground us, inspire us, and focus our minds on what we consider important. They can be done alone to calm the mind or with others to build intimacy and confirm the intention to Connect and be in recovery each day.

THE DECISION

Addictive thinking can be baffling, cunning, and devious. The Enlightened Brain can come up with any number of rationalizations and justifications for continuing Disconnected behavior. How do you know, then, what to do in all situations?

It is simple. Whatever the decision you have to make—whether it is what road to take to work, how to respond when your partner forgets an appointment, or how to behave in any situation—ask yourself this question:

Is this for my addiction or is this for my recovery?

Another way to understand this concept is to ask:

Will this cause me to Connect or will it cause me to Disconnect?

You will know the answer.

When you make decisions for your recovery, or Connection, you are controlling the one thing you can—yourself. If you make decisions that are for your addiction, or Disconnection, then you are trying to control something external and are setting yourself up for the resentment that leads to your addictive behavior. When that happens, everyone loses.

Whatever situation arises, you have a choice to be angry or to forgive, to push away or draw closer, to try to make someone else agree with you or to try to understand the other person. You can find any number of reasons to justify your choice, but it still comes down to that one question. How you answer it depends on what you really want for your life.

This one question, *"Does this cause me to Connect (recovery) or does it cause me to Disconnect (addiction)?"* has been the most valuable tool my clients have used and it is how I guide my own life.

Will this cause me to Connect or will it cause me to Disconnect?

Is this for my addiction or is this for my recovery?

CONNECTION MADE SIMPLE

A lot of ideas and suggestions have been presented in this book. I have tried to keep it as simple and straightforward as possible. In the end, though, I know that what people come away with is one single concept with which they can connect and hold on to. One simple idea that is easy to remember. So here it is: your "Recipe for Connection."

Be Like Sammi

Sammi is my dog, a cocker spaniel, to be precise. Quintessentially cute and the most loving dog you can find. My husband, Don, found her running down the middle of the road in the pre-dawn on his way to work. She was only about six weeks old. We never discovered where she came from, but she has been with us for eleven years now.

How does being like Sammi fit in with recovery and Connection? Let's see:

Sammi is completely in the moment. She has no preoccupations with the past and no worries about the future. Trust is not an issue because she has no doubts that her needs will be met. By being in the moment, Sammi enjoys whatever comes along—food, affection, a walk, or drive in the car—it's all good fun and she gets the most out of it every time.

Sammi expects to be loved. When she meets some-one new, she goes right to them, makes eye contact, wags what's left of her tail (it was docked when we found her), and waits to be petted. She doesn't worry about rejection or anyone's bad moods. She doesn't take it personally if she's ignored, just waits on the sidelines until someone pets her or says something nice and then she's right back in the picture. Never any hard feelings, ever.

Sammi asks for help when she needs it. If it's too difficult to jump into the van, she'll wait to be picked up. When there is thunder and she's scared, she'll come lay at our feet until it passes. When she falls into the canal because she got too excited about the ducks, she knows we'll fish her out and she's right back on the edge.

Sammi is loyal, stays by us, is always ready for a good time, and when she looks into our eyes, we feel only unconditional love.

Be like Sammi.

EPILOGUE

STORIES – PAST, PRESENT, AND FUTURE

"**H**i, I'm Carol and I'm an addict."

This is the introduction that millions of addicts around the world use when they stand up and share their stories with other addicts at twelve-step fellowship meetings such as Alcoholics Anonymous or Gamblers Anonymous. In a deeper sense, they are saying "I am admitting to my addiction, I am here because I want recovery, and I am like all of you. We are Connected."

Just like people sharing their life stories in fellowship meetings, telling my story to you allows me to Connect with you and for all of us to feel the commonality of our addiction—what it means, how it has affected us, and the hope of a better life in recovery.

When you write your own story, you will understand from where you came, you will be aware of yourself now, and you will discover where you want to be.

This is my story.

I was born in the state of Washington, but my parents divorced when I was only eight months old and my mother took me to live with her parents in New Jersey. In their old Victorian house, I had a wonderful first five years of life—all the unconditional love any child could wish for. I spent my days with my grandmother learning to play the piano and making pipe cleaner dolls with elaborate costumes; roaming through the attic with the flotsam and jetsam of bygone years and exploring the vast basement where my grandfather worked on mechanical drawings and engineering projects; walking to the corner of Main Street where I could meet my mother coming from the train station after a day at work. I had just started ballet classes when my life completely changed.

It all ended when I turned five and my mother married the man who would become my adopted father. She had the good intention of giving me a father, but as she sometimes said, the road to hell is paved with good intentions.

My father was a good man—intelligent, creative, and sensitive. He was an attorney for the government and never missed a day of work in his life. He was also an alcoholic. His early life, as it was and is and will be for so many, was shaped by a cold and domineering father for whom nothing was ever good enough and a mother whose focus must always be on her husband at the expense of her two sons. His drinking escalated when he returned from World War II while his brother, his father's favorite, was buried in the south of France. He was in his mid-thirties and leading a life of mostly solitary hunting and fishing when he married my mother, and our lives from then on revolved around him and his drinking. I went from being the center of the universe to some remote little planet of no importance. He did try, in the early years, to bond with me, but of course his drinking kept him from ever really connecting with me or knowing me. I will always appreciate, though, his willingness to adopt me and love me.

My parents had four more daughters, and I alternated between helping to care for them and going off on my own to read or ride my bike around town. I did adequately at school, but no one helped me with homework or gave me any guidance with negotiating the labyrinth of social relationships, so I was often lonely.

I left home before I even graduated high school, although I did finish. I bounced around from place to place, job to job, man to man, and had one long-term relationship with an alcoholic/drug addict, although I did not recognize the extent of his addictions at the time since my father could have drunk him under the table any day of the week.

It took some time, but after years of this rootless, directionless life, I eventually settled down and grounded myself. I began to realize that I must find within myself what I needed for a fulfilling life, and it was from that place of completeness, rather than need, that I fell in love with my husband, although we had known each other for many years. I had always been drawn to the helping professions and so I went to college for a bachelor's degree in psychology and then continued on to earn a graduate degree in counseling. It was while I was in the master's program that I realized how angry I was at my father and my ex-boyfriend, since I had the opportunity to take courses in substance abuse that would allow me to specialize in that area, but there was no way I was going to work with "those people!" I was *really* angry and did not want to let anyone off the hook for their hurtful behavior.

During the next few years, some interesting things happened. My ex-boyfriend called me out of nowhere and apologized for his meanness and emotional abuse while drinking and drugging. He was obviously working on the steps from his recovery program concerned with making amends to the people he had harmed. It was amazing how, as he took responsibility for his behavior and acknowledged my feelings, the old hurts dissolved and I felt validated and cared about.

My father also went into recovery from his alcoholism, although it was late in his life and the disease had cost him his health, his career, and his friends. I remember sitting in the visiting room of the rehab and for the first time in my life experiencing real warmth from him. I suddenly realized the barrier to intimacy and Connection that addiction creates. It was only in the absence of that barrier that I was aware of its past existence, as when one is only aware of the noise of an air conditioner when it stops.

At the same time that I was healing and letting go of the anger and hurt, I found myself looking for a counseling job in Miami, where we had moved soon after I graduated, and it was tough going for someone new to the field. I was finally accepted at—can you guess?—a drug rehabilitation program! I found myself doing individual and group therapy with addicts and their families and really learning about addiction from these experts, who were people with whom I could empathize and care about—something I was not willing to do before my own healing had begun.

Over the years, I began to realize how the pain and tragedy of addiction was also a gateway to a better life. I became aware that recovering people are forced to make decisions about the meaning of their lives and what is really important in life, which allows them to be more happy and content with themselves, more spiritually fulfilled and Connected with each other. I began to incorporate recovery principles into my own life, although recovery is a lifelong journey.

In time I acquired a certification in addictions and earned a doctoral degree in human sexuality. It seemed a logical step to make sex addiction a specialty. From there, I have come to realize that addiction is broader than any one drug or behavior. It is pervasive and subtle and infiltrates every aspect of our culture in America.

Finally, throughout my life, I have been on a spiritual journey as well. I was raised Presbyterian and later engaged in Buddhism and Kabbalah. My personal experiences have allowed me to grow spiritually, and this has enriched the counseling I provide to the incredibly diverse clients I see both here in Miami and by Internet around the world and also the lessons to the students in the university and institute where I teach. It is because I feel the need to share the truth of the insights and wisdom with which I have been blessed that I wrote this book.

What's your story? It's up to you to write the script for a new, Connected life.

APPENDIX

Substance Dependence

A maladaptive pattern of substance use leading to clinically significant impairment or distress, as manifested by three (or more) of the following, occurring any time in the same 12-month period:

1. Tolerance, as defined by either of the following:
(a) A need for markedly increased amounts of the substance to achieve intoxication or the desired effect
(b) Markedly diminished effect with continued use of the same amount of the substance.

2. Withdrawal, as manifested by either of the following:
(a) The characteristic withdrawal syndrome for the substance
(b) The same (or closely related) substance is taken to relieve or avoid withdrawal symptoms.

3. The substance is often taken in larger amounts or over a longer period than intended.

4. There is a persistent desire or unsuccessful efforts to cut down or control substance use.

5. A great deal of time is spent in activities necessary to obtain the substance, (e.g., visiting multiple doctors or driving long distances), use the substance (e.g., chain-smoking), or recover from its effects.

6. Important social, occupational, or recreational activities are given up or reduced because of substance use.

7. The substance use is continued despite knowledge of having a persistent physical or psychological problem that is likely to have been caused or exacerbated by the substance (for example, current cocaine use despite recognition of cocaine-induced depression or continued drinking despite recognition that an ulcer was made worse by alcohol consumption).

American Psychiatric Association: *Diagnostic and Statistical Manual of Mental Disorders*, Fourth Edition, Text Revision. Washington, DC, American Psychiatric Association, 2000.

BIBLIOGRAPHY

A Short History of Nearly Everything, Broadway; Ill Spl Re edition (October 5, 2010)

Alcoholics Anonymous: Big Book, AA Services (Author). Alcoholics Anonymous World Services (July 26, 2007)

American Psychiatric Association: Diagnostic and Statistical Manual of Mental Disorders, Fourth Edition, Text Revision. Washington, DC, American Psychiatric Association, 2000.

From Learning to Love: The Selected Papers of H.F. Harlow (Centennial Psychology Series) Clara Mears Harlow (Author). Publisher: Praeger Publishers (November 7, 1986)

Games People Play: The Basic Handbook of Transactional Analysis. Eric Berne (Author)

Man's Search for Meaning, Publisher: Beacon Press; 1 edition (June 1, 2006)

Overcoming Destructive Beliefs, Feelings, and Behaviors: New Directions for Rational Emotive Behavior Therapy, Albert Ellis (Author). Publisher: Prometheus Books (November 2001). Publisher: Ballantine Books; Seventh impression edition (August 27, 1996)

The Celestine Prophecy, James Redfield (Author). Publisher: Warner Books Inc. (November 1, 1997)

The Neurobehavioral and Social-Emotional Development of Infants and Children (Norton Series on Interpersonal Neurobiology), Ed Tronick (Author). Publisher: W. W. Norton & Company (July 31, 2007)

The Wind in the Willows, Kenneth Grahame (Author). Publisher: Puffin (March 27, 2008)

8431658R0

Made in the USA
Charleston, SC
08 June 2011